THE BEST JOKES

Minnie Pearl

EVER TOLD

(plus some that she overheard!)

THE BEST JOKES

Minnie Pearl

EVER TOLD

(plus some that she overheard!)

Compiled and written by

Kevin Kenworthy

THOMAS NELSON
Since 1798

NASHVILLE   DALLAS   MEXICO CITY   RIO DE JANEIRO

Published in Nashville, Tennessee, by Thomas Nelson. Thomas Nelson is a registered trademark of Thomas Nelson, Inc.

The name and likeness of Minnie Pearl are trademarks owned by the estate of Henry R. Cannon, which has authorized this use under license.

Typography by E. T. Lowe, Nashville, TN

Library of Congress Cataloging-in-Publication Data

Turner, Billy L., 1932–
    The best jokes that Minnie Pearl ever told / compilation and original
    materials by Billy L.Turner and Kevin A. Kenworthy.
        p.   cm.
    ISBN   978-1-55853-734-7   (pbk.)
        1. American wit and humor.   2. Minnie Pearl—Anecdotes.
    I. Kenworthy, Kevin A.   II. Title.
    PN6162.T87   1998   98-55327
    818'.5402—dc21   CIP

Printed in the United States of America

13 14 15 16 QG 19 18 17 16 15 14

Contents

Contents

Foreword

HOWDEE!

It's a simple signature. Yet the loud pronouncement brings the listener to attention and compels a choral response, "Howdee!" See. I told you! "I'm just so proud to be here!"

Many times I was lucky enough to join the choir of millions responding to Minnie's greeting. I sure miss yelling it out now that Minnie Pearl isn't here with us. I miss it because for me it meant a phone call almost every Friday afternoon. A call that was filled with laughs, groans, and just some good old chatting. "You're so bad!" was one of the most common responses I got from Miss Minnie. (That's what we called Minnie Pearl.) I would listen to her laughingly complain about the deadpan way I would read the volumes of jokes from which we would choose for our evening's segment on Ralph Emery's television show, *Nashville Now*, on The Nashville Network. Sure, I got groans in response to some of the less favorable entries, but the chatting was well worth wading through the seemingly endless punch lines.

Sometimes we would just "talk about the weather." Well, not literally, but it was the kind of talk that friends have. It was not prompted by anything more than just enjoying each other's company for a few minutes out of an otherwise busy day.

When I made my move from the Nation's Capital to Music City, (I obviously love living in cities that don't use their proper names), I didn't realize just how fortunate I would be transplanting myself to the heartland of country music. *Nashville Now* producer Bill Turner gave me as much latitude as he could when it came to the everyday material for TNN's flagship show, but like the best jokes, it was a good sense of timing that gave me my chance to laugh with comic nobility. Truthfully, it was really luck as well as timing that put me in charge of the weekly segments with Sarah Cannon, who as

Minnie Pearl was the Queen of Country Comedy. Almost every Friday I had *my* date with Minnie.

Now for most husbands this might have been perceived as a bad thing. Henry Cannon, her husband for fifty years, observed, "My wife seems to be spending a lot of time with this *other* man each week! Laughing, talking and when Minnie arrives to work the television show, this same guy follows her around like a puppy with his folder full of the evening's funny business." The folder usually contained three prize-winning tales that made their way through the grueling selection process and onto the air. But Henry Cannon never seemed to mind. In fact, he often reminded me of how much fun Minnie had when we spoke. I sure do miss those days.

Since a lot of my experience with her comedy resulted from my days working with Minnie at TNN, I guess I should tell you a little bit about how that whole deal worked. Once Minnie arrived on the set, she was escorted to the makeup trailer. "Lay it on 'cause this is as good as it gets on its own!" she would say. About that time, a crew or staff member would drop by my office in the next trailer or phone to tell me, "Miss Minnie has arrived!" That was generally my cue to drop everything less important, and everything was less important. "Sorry, Garth. I have to go now," I would say. Of course, he understood. Why, he named his firstborn after the comedienne. When Minnie was in the house, nothing else mattered.

Minnie generally greeted me with a sarcastic, yet loving, "Oh...there *he* is," which was followed by a general announcement to anyone else in the small room about what a bad joke teller I was. It didn't matter if it was Roy Acuff or Lorrie Morgan. I was treated like the star of a celebrity roast though I'd be lying if I didn't admit that I loved every minute of it.

After the show went on the air, the time arrived for the Queen to receive her subjects. I use the term *queen* in the same way that the whole world of Country Music does, not because she had a snooty attitude or air of over-importance. Heavens no! Quite the contrary! When Miss Minnie entered a room, she filled it with a feeling of royalty. Her crown was a straw hat. The prize jewel: a price tag on a string.

"Howdee!!"

You see! Caught yourself saying it back to her just now, didn't you? "I'm just so proud to be here!" This is how every Friday night segment started. That is where Minnie would shine, sitting with one of her favorite people, Ralph Emery, and in the living rooms of millions of fans. And me—well, I was probably standing nearby waiting for those moments when she would say my name to the audience. "Well, I'm not taking responsibility for this next joke. Kevin—you know he's the writer that helps me pick out jokes before the show—Oh! He's so bad! Oh! You should hear how bad he tells jokes!" she would say. "Well, he liked this one, so here goes nothin'!"

Thanks, Minnie. Those were my favorite moments of fame. Really.

Well, some of those jokes *were* bad, some were tired and old, and some were little funny bones just waiting to be tickled. But when blended together with some wonderfully crafted stories about Minnie's home, Grinder's Switch, and the cast of characters who occupied the sleepy little town, you have what we called a good time and a good laugh.

Sarah Cannon died March 4, 1996, but it's our luck that she left behind the legacy and stories of Minnie Pearl. I'm just glad that I was there to hear a lot of them for myself.

So, consider this to be your reader's advisory from someone who has personally experienced the comedy you're about to indulge. Before you sit around and haphazardly read all of these jokes and stories to your friends, be sure to get things off on the right foot. All you armchair Minnie Pearls need to slip on your Sunday gingham. Men, an appropriate summer suit with a whimsical tie will do. Next, blow the dust off a neatly adorned straw hat. Be sure to price it appropriately. A dollar and ninety-eight cents will do just fine, even with inflation.

Gather up all of your relations and friends in a circle, and then I think you know the word to say to get things rolling.

—Kevin Kenworthy

Acknowledgments

This book is dedicated to my wife, Danielle, who laughed, listened and fought the computer with me...and to the memory of my friend Minnie Pearl.

I also extend special thanks to Bill Turner, Ralph Emery and BJ plus all of Minnie's friends at the Opry and in Nashville who helped me find and remember these old stories.

THE BEST JOKES

Minnie Pearl
EVER TOLD
(plus some that she overheard!)

1.
Come On In!
The Water's Fine

If you came here looking for facts and figures, dates and statistics, shoe or hat size, you've come to the wrong place. That would be a biography of Sarah Cannon, and her character, Minnie Pearl. Walk on over and ask the librarian where that section is in the Dewey decimal registry. What you'll find in this book are stories about a quaint country town that was full of laughs, good folks and a place where trains decided which way they would go on Grinder's Switch. And you'll find lots of other jokes and tales that are just plain fun to tell.

Now, I don't profess to be an expert on Grinder's Switch. I don't think there ever was one, nor will there ever be one, with the possible exception of Minnie Pearl. I think Minnie was the closest thing the town will ever have to a bonafide historian. Truth is, and she'd probably agree, that maybe some of the stories that came out of that sleepy little crossing were slight exaggerations of the God's honest truth. She might say something like, "Well, if it isn't true, it oughta be!" And when you hear some of the tales that grew out of the Switch (that's what they called it for short) you might agree. So what exactly is the God's honest truth anyway? It's probably someone's best recollection of how they remember the story being told. And that's exactly what I've attempted to do here.

Now before you wander aimlessly into the Switch, you should brush up on your casual English. If you're a professor of the written word you might want to put on sunglasses and mittens to protect your literary integrity from an all-out country assault! You see, the spoken word in Grinder's Switch is what Brother might call "lazy man's wordin'." Don't be offended if by the time you reach the back cover you feel like your entire stock of the letter *g* has been heisted like the payroll off a stagecoach. I think if you look back in time you'll find that folks in the country just didn't feel it was necessary to expend the extra energy it takes to sometimes close a word with a resounding *g* sound. For example, if you live in the big city, you might expect to "go to a church and hear the choir singing a beautiful hymn." If you come from Grinder's Switch, you'd be more likely to "catch a pretty melody whilst the choir rendered up a mountain of singin'." See what I mean?

So, if you're so inclined and don't think you'll make it, by all means grab the nearest number two pencil and start scribblin' in the missin' *g*s throughout the following dialogues. I say use a pencil because by the time you get accustomed to the country style, you'll want to go back and erase all of your corrections and really hunker down for a good book readin'.

Another thing you probably need to know is that in a small town like Grinder's Switch, it's hard to light a candle without someone seeing the glow under your bushel basket. There are gossips and nosy neighbors aplenty. Of course, they all mean well. They'd be the first to tell you so. They're just communicating. Except the town's so small that their communication is as obvious as sending up smoke signals from inside a locked outhouse. It's pretty apparent to anyone nearby what your business is.

There are some sure-fired characters at Grinder's Switch. It's truly a town where the family acorns don't seem to fall far from the tree! Minnie's family, as I know it, consisted of a few key individuals. Don't worry, I'll help you with the hard names.

Some of the names of Minnie's immediate family—Mammy, Brother, and Sister—are pretty self-explanatory and are pronounced very much the way they look. They were a fairly proper bunch, and Brother always seemed to end up on the short end of every rake handle. But it was his commitment to underachievement and general good ol' boyishness that produced some of the best tales of the Switch. Minnie also talks frequently about her Uncle Nabob and Aunt Ambrosia. Let's step back for a second and go over those names.

If you can, go outside and lean against a picket fence with a blade of grass properly perched 'tween your teeth, or sit on a porch swing and go to it while you practice these. You see, Nabob is pronounced "Nay-bob." As for the spelling, well, there are differing opinions that don't have the slightest connection as to how the name is pronounced. Don't be embarrassed if your neighbor hears you brushing up on your down-home articulations. Just tell them that you're rehearsing for *Oklahoma*. Now for Aunt Ambrosia, you might want to hold on to something when you say this one because when uttered properly it flies out of your mouth like a greased pig loose at the county fair. The proper way to say this name is "Am-bro-zee!" Go ahead now and practice, "Aunt Am-bro-zee." When you start feeling really confident, and maybe a little brazen, combine the two relatives in the same phrase "Uncle Nay-bob and Aunt Am-bro-zee!" If you need to take a break and "set a spell" after doing this exercise, I won't take offense.

Assuming you've caught your breath and don't have a headache from the stress of relearning the language you grew up with, let's move on. You'll find a lot of other colorful people in Grinder's Switch: old Doc Payne, the town physician; Moonshine McGinny, the town lush; Mad Mountain Murdock, the blacksmith and man of definitive stature; and of course Poker Face Perkins—you can figure that one out on your own. You'll find many more inhabitants of this little burg, but I don't want to entirely take away the element of surprise.

I'm sure accounts of life at the Switch continue to grow as time goes by. Everyone assumes that these folks didn't uproot and move to the big city. Life goes on. But I've got to start you off on your comic expedition from somewhere, set a benchmark of sorts. Except, unlike other adventurers, you have the advantage of knowing that the world is a round place.

I've conveyed the stories I actually remember being told by Minnie in the first person because that's how she would have told them to you. They're mostly mini-chronicles that have been brought back to my attention by friends or ones that I recalled. Now you might have heard them differently, but like I said earlier, "If they ain't the truth, they oughta be." And as you run through the tales of Grinder's Switch and you've got up a good head of steam, keep reading. The other comic treasures included are little niblets from the old archive of jokes Minnie and I used to tell to each other. I've also sprinkled in the recollections of some of her cronies. If you know Minnie, then I think you'll recognize their names when you see them.

Just remember that even if it's not indicated, when you're reading those extra morsels leave off a few *g*s and throw in a *Howdee!* or two just for flavor. You'll be surprised how much funnier they become.

2.
Porter Wagoner Remembers Minnie

While Minnie Pearl and Roy Acuff reigned as country music's royalty, there were many noble dignitaries who shared in the spotlight of such legends including perennial crowd favorite, Porter Wagoner. Porter is one star who helped sling the country lifestyle out of the cornfields and hillsides right onto Main Street with his successful television career. Since Minnie and Roy's departure, he has seemingly filled the void as the Grand Ole Opry's leading man. It is a well-earned position as Porter also served as Opryland's Ambassador while the theme park stood in Music City.

Porter himself is no stranger to getting a hearty laugh on stage. The tall, lean country gentleman, like so many great entertainers, has carefully crafted his blend of music and comedy. His act is enhanced by a flashy wardrobe and hidden message in his coattails for the crowd. He passed on to me one of his favorite stories that Minnie told, and one which he has also performed on stage many times himself. "I always give her credit for it, because it was one of her really great stories," Porter willfully divulged. The account dabbles in the sanctity of a lasting marriage. Chances are it happened in Grinder's Switch.

There was an old couple who were celebrating their fiftieth wedding anniversary. That night they were lying in bed,

reminiscing back over their fifty years of happiness. And the lady said to her husband, "Honey, do remember what you done fifty years ago tonight?" He said, "Gosh no, what?" She said, "Well, you put your arm around me and held me real close." And so he did it. He put his arm around her and held her up real close. She then said, "You know what else you done fifty years ago tonight?" He said, "No, what?" She said, "You kissed me on the cheek!" Well, he pulled her over and gave her a nice kiss. Then she said to him, "Do you remember what else you done fifty years ago tonight?" He said, "No, what?" She said, "You bit me right here on the ear!" Just then the old guy jumped up and flew out of bed and started running across the room! His wife said, "Wait a minute, honey! What are you doing? Where are you going?" He said, "I'm gonna go get my teeth!"

As Minnie was a prolific storyteller, Porter didn't stop with just one narrative. He shared this bonus dispatch with me. It was one, he confessed, that he had Minnie tell to him several times a year. Better give the horse an extra carrot because it's a long road but well worth the drive!

Back in Grinder's Switch there was a lady on welfare who lived way out in the country, and she had fourteen children. So, the town welfare lady went out to her house one day to pay a visit and talk to her about having so many children. When the welfare lady drove up to the house there were kids just everywhere! Some of them were looking out the window, some of them under the porch, and some on the porch with their momma. Shocked, the welfare lady walked up and said, "Ma'am, I came out to talk to you about your welfare check. You're getting the maximum that anybody can get; you have fourteen children and I notice that they're just barely getting by. You're gonna have to stop having kids! I also know that you've been married fourteen years and you've got fourteen kids. You're just gonna have to put a stop to it!" And the lady said, "Well, I'll do my best. Can you help me out in any way?"

And the welfare lady said, "I'll tell you what you can do. You get you a ten-gallon butter churn and sleep with your feet in it." And the lady said, "Beg your pardon?" "Get you a butter churn and sleep with your feet in it," said the welfare lady.

With that, the welfare lady went on back to town. She waited almost a year to go back out to see how the woman and her fourteen children were doing. When she drove up to the house it was almost the same scene as the last time she visited. Kids were at the window, under the porch, on the porch, and out in the yard. And like before, the lady was sitting on the front porch now rocking number fifteen. The welfare lady was astounded and went up on the porch and said, "Ma'am, I can't believe this! I don't know what to say to you! I told you the last time that you were getting the maximum and you were gonna have to stop having kids, but here you are with number fifteen!" The lady said, "Well, you told me to get a ten gallon churn and sleep with my feet in it. But I couldn't find a ten-gallon churn. So, I got two five-gallons and slept with a foot in each one!"

3.
Tyin' Ourselves Up in Knots

Marriage is the perfect institution, and relationships always bloom eternal. I think that roughly translates into "marriage can lead you to the nuthouse, and relationships often blossom into wars of wisdom."

Every relationship certainly has its share of give-and-take. However, in some cases what you're left with after you've been taken isn't enough to fill a snuff tin. Nonetheless, men and women seem content to pursue love no matter the cost. Look at the timeless romantics throughout history: Romeo and Juliet, Antony and Cleopatra, Minnie Pearl and Hezzie. Yes, Minnie and Hezzie.

You see, Minnie was a hopeless romantic, and Hezzie...well, let's just say that he seemed hopeless. He never quite won the fifty-yard dash to the altar but always had the best intentions. Oh sure, it seemed like Minnie never missed a handsome face in the crowd, but she was ever faithful to her true love, Hezzie. Kind of like Sarah Cannon and her husband, Henry. Except to Henry's credit, he won the dash and tied the knot.

Now remember, Grinder's Switch is a small town. So, beware lovers wherever you are and no matter how old you are because the walls have ears and the windows have watchers. (Sigh!) Love. One day you're single, the next day Cupid has seen through that cheap camouflage you bought at a yard sale and stuck you with his arrow.

You might as well step out from your duck blinds, fellows, because it's inevitable that we can't live with love, and we can't live without it.

* * *

Ain't this April weather just grand? April is the month the girls start thinkin' about bridal showers and the fellers get April foolish. We had a birthday party for Brother 'cause April Fools' Day is his birthday. Every year it's so convenient that he was born on April Fools' Day 'cause every dog has his day and Brother has April Fools' Day.

I sure hope this is one spring that winds up in a wedding. For me! I reckon one of these days my feller, Hezzie, will take me for better or for worse. That'll be when, if he can't do any better, and I can't do any worse!

It's a funny thing when a feller takes a girl out for a drive in his car. He always knows where to park, but he never knows when to stop. But, it's like my Aunt Rosie always says, "A little parkin' every now and then makes husbands out of single men!" I remember one time I was out ridin' with Hezzie, and we heard a girl in a parked car hollerin', "Stop! Stop!" Well, we thought it was a holdup! So, when the girl hollered stop, Hezzie jammed on his brakes, grabbed a monkey wrench and started over to the car. When he got there, that girl stuck her head out the window and said, "Keep goin', Buster. I wasn't talkin' to you!"

* * *

Well I just read in the paper about one of the most thoughtful and considerate women I've ever heard of. She shot her husband with a bow and arrow so as not to wake the younguns.

* * *

We had us our annual Amateur Contest at Grinder's Switch last night. They had all kinds of talent there. And I was there too. And Lizzie Twitchem, well she done a dance. She's that girl with an hourglass figure, and she certainly makes every second count.

And then they had a band. It was a fine mountain music

Minnie Pearl, was a lighthearted and delightful country lady representing the best of Grinder's Switch, as seen here in this early 1940s publicity photo.

Courtesy of Les Leverett

band, yes indeed. Uncle Nabob was playin' the jug, and everybody was so pleased with how well he was playin' the jug. Can't nobody get more out of a jug than Uncle Nabob!

And Mad Mountain Murdock—he was the hit of the show that Mad Mountain Murdock. He done his strongman act. He lifted a platform that had the whole Wilkers family on it: Jessie and Lucy and eight younguns right on there! Everybody was exclaimin' about how wonderful it was, him liftin' all that. He said, "That ain't nothin'; I've been supportin' my wife's family now for years!"

* * *

From Minnie's advice column in the Grinder's Switch newspaper:

Dear Minnie,

When my boyfriend calls on me he doesn't want to do anything but sit in the parlor and kiss me from eight o'clock 'til twelve. Do you think we spend too much time on kissin?

Signed,
Puzzled

Dear Puzz,

Them's the kind of puzzles I enjoy workin' on personal. But I've always found that kissin's like eatin' soup with a fork. It takes a long time to get enough!

*

Dear Minnie,

My husband says I've been puttin' on too much weight, and if I don't reduce he'll leave me. Didn't he promise to love me for better or for worse?

Signed,
Punkins

Dear Punk,

Better take it off. He promised to love you through better or for worse but not through thick and thin!

*

Dear Minnie,

I have two men that are crazy about me and one is rich and handsome and drives a big beautiful car, and his name is Henry. The other one is poor and not so good lookin', and his name is Joe. What should I do?

Signed,
Undecided

Dear Undie,

By all means marry the poor boy. P.S. Send me the address and phone number of Henry!

(I'm sure it was just a coincidence that this man's name was Henry!)

* * *

I don't have to worry about no fellers chasin' me as long as I've got my Hezzie. I'll have you know that Hezzie is a lover of the "old school." Sometimes I wish he'd get past the fourth grade, though!

But you know, Hezzie and I were out one night, and we come upon this real pretty little girl sittin' out on her front steps, and she had a little cat in her arms. When Hezzie come by her he started strokin' that cat's fur. He said to me, "Look! When I stroke this cat's fur the wrong way you can see the sparks fly!" And I said to Hezzie, "If you don't confine your strokes to that *cat* you're gonna see the fur fly!"

* * *

My boyfriend Hezzie came over the other night to sort of set a spell with me and keep me company. It was a warm autumn night and we was sittin' there in the front room and it was so romantical. It was late. It musta been eight-thirty! We was sittin' there and all of a sudden he got red in the face and started squirmin' around and wipin' his brow, and I said to myself, "This is it! Hezzie's a fixin' to propose to me." Oh, I was so excited I didn't know what to do. I wanted to help him out, so I said, "Come on, Hezzie, it's later than you think!" And he said, "That ain't it, Minnie. It's just too early for this long panel underwear!"

* * *

Most folks in Grinder's Switch, they get along pretty good. Like Lucifer Hucklehead and his wife—he says that she's just perfect for him. He says that when his wife's out in the field, she can pull corn and act as a scarecrow all at the same time!

* * *

I always hear fellers complain about what a hard time they have. You know what my mammy always says? She says, "Anytime you hear a feller complainin' about leadin' a dog's life, it just means one thing. He growls in the morning, barks in the afternoon, and wants to go out every night!"

* * *

A feller come a lookin' for Uncle Nabob the other day and asked Aunt Ambrosia where he could find him. Aunt Ambrosia said, "Just walk down to the creek 'til you come to a fishin' pole with a worm on each end!"

It seemed that she was mad with Uncle Nabob 'cause him and two other fellers had been out the night before and the next morning Aunt Ambrosia said to Uncle Nabob, "Look at you! Just look at you! Your old eyes are all bloodshot!" He said, "If you think they look bloodshot from there, you oughta see 'em from this side!"

* * *

A young feller friend of mine asked me could he give me some advice. I told him he didn't seem old enough to give sensible advice to a young girl like me. I told him, "Uncle Nabob says that the only time a pretty girl can trust a man is when the man is so old his eyes are on their last leg!"

He gave me the advice anyway. He told me I should keep the fellers guessin'. I said, "Well, I do keep the fellers guessin'. Why just today I passed two fellers on the street and they looked at me in such a peculiar way." He asked me how that proved that I keep the fellers guessin'. I said, "Well, I heard one of the fellers say to the other one,'What do you guess that was?' " Then he told me I should be more distant, more aloof, more poised. I said, "You mean if I have more poise I'll get more boys?" And he said, "Be a little cooler. Treat the men indifferently." I told him, "Oh, I treat the men indifferently. I treat 'em just like dirt. Every night I look under the bed for 'em!"

* * *

I was tellin' a friend about how my feller Hezzie is so thoughtful and so generous. "Why he gave me a mink outfit the other day," I told her. She said, "What was it? A mink cape and a muff?" I told her, "No. It was two traps and a gun."

* * *

A man and his wife went back to the place where they spent their honeymoon to celebrate their fiftieth wedding anniversary.

That night when they started to retire for the evening, the woman noticed tears running down her husband's cheeks.

She said, "Why Honey! I had no idea that you were so sentimental!" He replied, "I was just thinking about the night that your father caught us fooling around down at the barn. I remember him saying that if I didn't marry you, he'd see that I spent fifty years in jail, and I was just thinking that today I would be a free man!"

✳ ✳ ✳

One Saturday night a man walked into a bar, sat down on a stool, and quickly said to the bartender, "Gimme a double shot of whiskey!" He immediately drank it down, then he looked into his shirt pocket. After that, he ordered another double and drank it down. Once again, he looked into his shirt pocket, then ordered another double.

After about an hour of ordering and drinking about eight doubles and looking in his shirt pocket after each drink, the bartender finally asked, "Why do you drink down the double and then look in your shirt pocket?" He slurred, "I have a picture of my wife in there, and when she starts to look good, it's time to go home!"

✳ ✳ ✳

There's this man who lives out on the edge of town who's married to a four-hundred-pound woman who nags and henpecks him all the time, and she's always waiting with the frying pan if he comes home late or forgets to do a chore. One night he lost track of time, and was returning home in the wee hours of the morning. When he got to his house, he found a burglar jimmying the lock on his back door. The burglar jumped up and turned to the man and said, "Don't get any closer! I've got a billy club, and I know how to use it!" Knowing his wife was inside waiting with the frying pan he thought quickly and said to the burglar, "Listen, I'll unlock the door for you if you'll go in first!"

✳ ✳ ✳

A beautiful funeral was in progress for a man who had just passed away. The country preacher talked at great length about the good traits of the deceased. "He was an honest man, a loving husband, and a good and kind father."

Just then his widow leaned over to one of her kids and said, "Run up there and take a look in that coffin and make sure that's your pa in there!"

* * *

A man raced hurriedly into a drugstore with a worried look on his face and asked the druggist, "Do you know a way to stop the hiccups?" Without warning the druggist slapped the man upside the head. The man was shocked and angry and demanded that the druggist explain his actions immediately! "Well," said the druggist, "you don't have the hiccups now, do you?" "No," answered the man, "but my wife out in the car still does!"

* * *

At two in the morning, a man and his wife were sleeping soundly when they were awakened by the ringing of the telephone. The wife said, "John, get up and answer that!" So, John got up quietly and not quite awake went to answer the telephone. After a short time, he returned grumbling to himself. "Who was it?" asked his wife. "Oh," said John, "just some kook wanting to know if the coast was clear!" Slowly the wife asked, "Well, what did you tell him?" John said, "I told him, 'How the heck do I know! The coast is twenty miles from here!'"

* * *

A young man came home from work and found his inexperienced bride crying and upset. "I feel terrible!" she said. "Why?" he asked. "I was pressing your suit and I burned a big hole in the seat of your trousers," she said.

"Oh! Is that all? Just forget about it," consoled her husband. "Didn't you remember that I've got an extra pair of pants for that suit?" "Yes, I did," said the woman, cheering up a bit. "And it's lucky you do. I used them to patch the hole!"

* * *

One day a young man named Jack Small set off to the post office to mail a package to his sweetheart for Valentine's Day. He wasn't really sure that he had made the right choice, so he told the postman who said to Mr. Small, "Why, haven't you heard? Every woman knows that good things come in small packages!"

* * *

There were three men waiting outside a hospital delivery room. After awhile, a nurse came into the waiting room and said, "Congratulations, Mr. Brown, you're the father of twins!" "Well, what a coincidence," said Mr. Brown. "I work for the Minnesota Twins baseball team!"

Soon the nurse came into the waiting room again and said, "Congratulations, Mr. Green! You're the father of triplets!" "Well, what a coincidence," said Mr. Green. "I work for the 3-M Corporation!"

The third man in the waiting room got up from his chair and started to leave. The nurse saw him and said, "Wait, sir, you can't go yet. Your wife hasn't delivered! Why are you leaving now?" The man turned around and said, "I'm going to find a second job because I work for the 7-Up Company!"

* * *

There was a band leader who frequently got requests to play a song in honor of someone's wedding anniversary. He got a laugh when a young couple announced their first anniversary and he played "Night and Day." Another couple bragged that it was their fifth anniversary, so he played "Saturday Night."

This went on all evening. For a tenth he played, "Once in a While." For a twenty-fifth, "Now and Then." Thinking that he had run out of songs, a couple celebrating their fiftieth anniversary was serenaded with "Thanks for the Memories!"

When he asked, "Anyone here celebrating more than fifty years?" An elderly man in the back yelled, "Yes! How about playing, 'Never in a Million Years!' "

A married woman told her psychiatrist, "Doctor, I cheated on my husband six times in one night and haven't been able to sleep since!" The doctor told her, "Go home and drink the juice of six lemons." "Will that help me to sleep?" she asked. "No," replied the doctor, "but it will help wipe that silly grin off your face!"

* * *

A timid little henpecked fisherman had been advised by his psychiatrist to go home and assert himself. "Don't let your wife bully you around anymore," said the doctor. "Go home and let her know who's boss!" So the shy man went home, swung the front door open, and said in a loud voice, "Now get this, from now on I'm the boss of this house and I'm giving the orders and you're obeying them! Now get my supper on the table then lay out my fishing clothes, 'cause I'm going fishing! And do you know who's gonna dress me in my fishing clothes?" "Yes, dear," said his wife softly, "the undertaker."

* * *

There were three buddies out on the town when at three o'clock in the morning they were in a terrible car accident and all three were killed. They arrived at the gates of heaven where they were met by Saint Peter, who told them they would have to answer a few questions before entering.

The first man who answered was doing real well until Saint Peter asked him the last question, "Were you ever unfaithful to your wife?" The man thought awhile and said, "Yes, quite a few times." So Saint Peter thought a bit and handed him a set of keys to an old Volkswagen to drive around in heaven.

Courtesy of Les Leverett

You've heard all about Grinder's Switch, so, here it is with the town's favorite resident Minnie Pearl, taking a leisurely stroll down the tracks.

The second man was asked the same questions by Saint Peter, and he also was asked if he had ever been unfaithful to his wife. He answered right away, "Yes, but only one time." Saint Peter thought a bit and handed him a set of keys to a Buick to get around in heaven.

The third man was asked the same questions and he also was asked if he had ever been unfaithful to his wife. "No, no, never!" he told Saint Peter. So Saint Peter immediately handed him a set of keys to a brand new Cadillac to drive around in heaven.

A week later the first and second man were driving down the road together and came upon the third man parked along the side of the road leaning over the steering wheel of his Cadillac crying his eyes out. They stopped and asked if there was anything they could do to help. He looked up with tears in his eyes and said "No, not really." One of them asked, "Well, what's wrong?" The man replied, "I just saw my wife go by on a skateboard!"

* * *

A man and his wife were at a swanky, buffet-style dinner party in town when the wife whispered to her hubby, "That's the fifth time you've gone back for more chicken. Doesn't that embarrass you?" He said, "Not at all. I keep telling 'em I'm getting it for my wife."

* * *

A man's wife awakened one morning with an excruciating pain in her back. Her husband brought her breakfast in bed and a heating pad and left for work giving strict instructions that she should stay in bed. By midmorning, and about the time when a neighbor telephoned to say she was desperate for a fourth for her bridge club luncheon, her back was so much better that she agreed to fill in.

While enjoying the afternoon of bridge she had almost completely forgotten about her back until she saw her neighbor's husband coming home from work. With a start she realized that her husband would be home soon too! So she jumped up and grabbed her purse just as her friend's husband walked in. "I can't believe it's that late!" she cried. "I've got to go home and get in bed before my husband gets home." Her friend's husband sighed, "Now that's the kind of wife I always wanted."

* * *

One day two men met on the street. One of them was wearing a pair of ladies' panty hose. The other guy said, "Why on earth are you wearing panty hose and when did you start wearing them?" The other man answered, "Ever since my wife found them in the glove compartment of my car."

* * *

A man and his wife had saved up for years to go spend their vacation at the beautiful Sand and Sea Resort. It was a very pricey place and when it was time to check out, the man noticed some peculiar items on his bill. He asked the desk clerk, "What's this fifty-dollar daily charge for fruit? We didn't eat any." The clerk said, "But the fruit was placed in your room every day. It isn't our fault you didn't take advantage of it." "I see," said the man. So he grabbed a pen from the clerk and proceeded to subtract $150 off of the bill. "What do you think you're doing?" sputtered the clerk. The man said, "I'm subtracting fifty dollars a day off of my bill for you kissing my wife." The clerk said, "What? I didn't kiss your wife!" The man replied, "Yeah, but she was there. You just didn't take advantage of it!"

* * *

A man and his wife were watching *Jeopardy* on television when the wife asked her husband, "What would you say if Alex Trebek came up to our door and said 'Let me take you away from all of this!' " The husband replied, "What is: Where are you going with my wife?"

* * *

A married couple, both avid golfers, were discussing the future one night. "Honey," the wife said, "if I were to die, and you were to remarry, would the two of you live in this house?" The husband said, "I suppose so. It's paid for." "Well, how about my car?" the wife asked. "Would you let her drive my car?" He said, "I suppose so. It's paid for too." Finally she asked, "What about my set of golf clubs? Would you let her use them too?" Her husband blurted out, "Heck no! She's left-handed!"

* * *

Mary loved John, but she worried about the way he squandered money on her when they went out together. Finally, she consulted her mother. She asked, "Mom, how can I stop John from spending so much money on me?" Her mother said, "Marry him!"

* * *

One night at a party a woman accused a man at the next table of being disgustingly drunk. He replied, "And you're disgustingly ugly! But tomorrow morning *I'll* be sober." A few weeks later they met again under similar circumstances, and she again accused him of being disgustingly drunk. She said, "If I was your wife I would put poison in your coffee!" He replied, "Lady, if I was your husband, I'd drink it!"

* * *

A porter, loaded down with suitcases, followed a married couple to the airline check-in counter. As they approached the line, the husband glanced at the huge pile of luggage and said to his wife, "Are you sure you didn't bring the piano with you, too?" She laughed and said, "I know you're just trying to be funny, aren't you?" "No," he sighed, "I left the tickets on it."

* * *

A couple was having a yard sale on a really hot summer day. So the husband stretched out on a lounge chair and unexpectedly fell asleep. When he awoke he heard people laughing and found that while he was asleep, his wife had placed a sign at his feet which read, "Make me an offer."

* * *

Two men died and went to heaven. While they were waiting for Saint Peter to let them through the Pearly Gates, they began talking to each other. The first man asked, "So what did you die from?" The second man said, "I froze to death." The first man said, "That must have been terrible." The second man said, "It was. Your hands and feet get real cold, you shake all over, and then you finally die. What did you die from?" The first man said, "I had a heart attack. One day I came home early from work, walked into the house, and the table was set with a candlelit dinner for two and that's when I saw my wife run out of the bedroom wearing a negligee. I knew then and there that she had another man. So I looked all over the house. First downstairs then upstairs, then I went down into the basement but couldn't find anyone. Then I started running back up the stairs to the second floor and that's when it happened. I had a massive heart attack and died." The second man quietly said, "If you would have looked in the deep freezer, you could have saved us both!"

* * *

A young mother enlisted the help of a friend in taking her identical infant twins to the doctor. Since the waiting area was full, the two women, each with a twin, were seated on opposite sides of the room. After a few minutes someone who came in later commented, "It's amazing how much your two babies look alike." The friend was quick to reply, saying, "Well, they should. They have the same father!"

* * *

A husband was out in the field with his children trying to get a kite in the air, but to no avail. He would run with it to get it airborne, but it would just fall straight back to the ground. Just then, along came his wife, who watched for a few minutes and remarked, "What you need is a little more tail!" Her husband stopped and looked at her and said, "I wish you'd make up your mind. Last night you told me to go fly a kite!"

* * *

Mr. Smith, a seventy-five-year-old multimillionaire, just married a young, beautiful eighteen-year-old girl. A friend asked, "How did you get an eighteen-year-old to marry you when you're seventy-five?" The man said, "I told her I was ninety-five!"

* * *

A sixteen- and seventeen-year old decided that they were in love and just had to get married, much to the opposition of their parents. When the minister asked the youthful bride and groom to repeat after him, "With all my worldly goods I thee endow," the mother of the groom nudged her husband and whispered, "There goes his bike."

* * *

There were two men who got stuck playing golf behind two slow women on the front nine. As the two women were holding up their game, one of the men told the other to go up and tell the two women to hurry it up. The man got about halfway towards them, turned around, and came running back. "What's wrong?" asked the other man. He said. "Well, one was my wife and the other was my mistress. You go tell them to hurry it up." The other man got halfway towards them and he too came back in a hurry. "What's wrong?" asked the first man. He answered, "Small world, isn't it?"

* * *

Two happily married couples and one unhappily married couple all went to breakfast one morning. After being seated, the first happily married man said to his wife, "Pass the sugar, Sugar." The second happily married man said to his wife, "Pass the honey, Honey." The unhappily married man, realizing that he should say something, turned to his wife and said, "Pass the bacon, Piggy."

* * *

Many years ago, a farmer was helping at the delivery of his latest offspring by holding a kerosene lantern. When the doctor had produced not one, but *two* fine babies, the farmer screamed and bolted out of the room. "Come back with the lantern!" the doctor shouted. "I will not!" was the answer. "It's the light that's attracting them!"

* * *

A woman complained to the builder of her new house, "When trains go by, the vibration practically shakes me out of bed. Lie in the bed and see for yourself!"

As the builder settled onto her bed, the woman's husband suddenly appeared in the bedroom doorway. "Just what do you think you're doing?" he roared.

The embarrassed builder replied, "Would you believe waiting on a train?"

* * *

A man went to a psychiatrist because he was worried about his wife. "She's got this horrible fear that her clothes will be stolen," he told the doctor. "How can you tell?" asked the psychiatrist. The husband answered, "Well, the other day when I got home early from work, I found out that she had hired a man to stand in the closet and guard them!"

* * *

One morning at the breakfast table, a husband was looking over the stock market in the morning edition. At the same time his wife was telling him about the latest diet that she had tried and had failed with. With that her husband looked up from the stock quotes and said, "You know, Honey, you're the only investment I've ever made that's doubled!"

* * *

Two employees, who were also friends, arrived at work at the same time. The one said hello to the other who just grunted back. The first asked, "Did you wake up grouchy this morning?" The second man answered, "No, I let her wake up by herself."

* * *

A man took the hand of his fiancée in his and gazed proudly at the engagement ring that he had given her only three days before. "Did your friends admire it?" he asked tenderly. She said, "They did more than that. Two of them recognized it!"

A couple was having a heated discussion regarding the family finances. Finally, the wife exploded and yelled, "If it weren't for my money, this television set wouldn't be here. If it weren't for my money, that easy chair you're sitting in wouldn't be here either! And if it weren't for my money, this house wouldn't be here!" "Are you kidding?" the husband snorted. "If it weren't for your money, *I* wouldn't be here!"

* * *

A salesman, who was scheduled to come home on Friday, covered his territory in record time and sent his wife a telegram that read, "Will be home Thursday." Arriving home on Thursday he parked his car and walked up to the house only to see through the picture window his wife in the arms of another man. Instead of entering his house, the irate husband went down the block to see his father-in-law and told him the whole story.

"I'm not going to stand for this!" he shouted. "I'm going to file for a divorce in the morning." His father-in-law replied, "Now don't be hasty. I'm sure there must be a good explanation. Let me go down and talk to her." So the father went to his daughter's house, came back, and said, "I knew there'd be a good reason. She didn't get your telegram!"

* * *

At a local bar, a young woman was expounding on her idea of the perfect mate to some of her friends. "The man I marry must be a shining light amongst company. He must be musical. Tell jokes. Sing. And stay home at night!"

A cynical male listener overheard and spoke up, "Lady, what you really want is a television set!"

* * *

A young boy was taking a girl to a dance for the first time. His mother, noting his nervousness, instructed him in the proper social graces. "Remember," she said, "she'll be just as nervous

In radio's heyday, a character was built on the things that they said and the way that they said them. But Minnie Pearl dressed the part whenever and wherever she was performing.

Courtesy of Les Leverett

as you are so say something nice to set her at ease." Later on while they were dancing, the boy remembered what his mother had told him and finally said, "Boy! For a fat girl you sure don't sweat much!"

* * *

An old country farmer went into the hardware store in town to buy an air conditioner for his wife. The salesman asked if he could help him. "Yes, I'm looking for an air conditioner," the farmer said. The salesman began to explain that he had a 12,000 Btu unit, a 15,000 Btu unit, until the farmer looked at the salesman and interrupted, "Look here. I don't know anything about these Btus. I just want an air conditioner big enough to cool a B.U.T. as big as a T.U.B!"

* * *

A woman accompanied her husband when he went to the doctor for his annual checkup. While the man was getting dressed, the doctor came out and said to the wife, "I don't like the way your husband looks." To which she replied, "Neither do I, but he's so handy around the house."

* * *

A young couple in love were walking out across the pasture to be alone. When they got to the back pasture fence, they sat down. He started to tell her how much and sincere his love for her was. "Honey, I will face death for you," he promised.

On their way home, a bull that had been grazing in the field started to chase them. Running for their lives, they rolled under the fence just in time. Out of breath, the young lady looked over at the young man and said, "I thought you said you would face death for me?" "Yes," he said, "but that bull wasn't dead!"

* * *

A man went to the doctor for a checkup. After the examination, the doctor said, "There's nothing wrong with you. All you need is a little sun and air." The patient answered, "Gee Doctor, I just got married. We can't afford a son and heir yet."

* * *

A man returned home from work one night to find the whole house in a terrible mess. Astounded, he asked his wife what had happened. "You always ask me what I do all day," she said. "Well, now you know. I didn't do it today!"

4.
Wooin' and Cooin'

I have to confess that even way out in the country there are wolves and foxes, not the kind you're thinking of but the kind that walk on *two* legs. I'm sure you've encountered them. They're the wolves out working in a field or on a tractor that start whistling "Dixie" any time a cute little fox crosses their path.

Well, even in Grinder's Switch the wildlife seems to have made its way inside the city limits. Now, keep in mind that at the Switch girls are to be proper and men are to be, well, kept at arm's length. It's a town where courting doesn't mean suing your neighbor because his pit bull ate your Chihuahua, or where shining and mooning don't mean a bald man has decided to play a fraternity prank on his buddies. It's just a town where good old playfulness is a way of life, and loving your neighbor is just a figure of speech.

It's also a place where the Bikini Islands are still a tropical getaway and not cars full of college coeds on spring break at the beach. Why, the ladies of Grinder's Switch wouldn't be caught dead wearing some of the skimpy costumes you find on girls today. No sir, It's a town where "bear" skin is something you cover up with. Still, the men there aren't immune to the siren's call of a lovely young maiden, and in their defense, the single women haven't lost their touch when it comes to stringing a man along.

✳ ✳ ✳

I got a postcard from my Aunt Abigail in Florida. She's my maiden aunt, and she's got a little bit of money. She summers at Niagara Falls, winters at Miami Beach, and springs at men!

Aunt Abby's postcard was from one of the hotels where she was stayin' and it said, "The men at this hotel have been grabbin' girls in dark hallways and kissin' them! So I had to complain to the manager. Not one of 'em tried to kiss me!"

* * *

This afternoon when I left Grinder's Switch down there where I live at, my friend Lizzy Tinkem said, "Oh, I sure do envy you goin' up to the Grand Ole Opry every Saturday night where all them handsome fellers are. Now if you see some really handsome fellers up there tonight, you flirt with 'em just for me, hear?"

So when I got to the Opry I saw Grant Turner. So I flirted a little with Grant. I did it for Lizzy, of course, not for me. Then I saw old Ernie Newton, and I kinda flirted with him for Lizzy, not for me. But when I seen that Rex Allen, that's when I decided to go into business for myself!

* * *

I'm just plum tickled. I just got kissed by a feller with a big, bushy mustache. Now I don't want any of you thinkin' that I'm one of those weak-willed people. Fact is my will is stronger than my won't! But this here feller that kissed me apologized. He said it was a hobby of his—goin' around kissin' beautiful women. He was so tall, and so handsome... and so nearsighted!

Brother said to me, "You mean to tell me that you were kissed by a perfect stranger?" I told him, "Brother, nobody's perfect!" He said, "I just can't imagine you letting a strange man kiss you." I told him right then and there he had no imagination! Then he asked, "Didn't you resist him? Didn't you repulse him?" I told him, "Of course I did! You ought to have seen me try to repulse him. Why no girl could ever have been so repulsive!"

Then he asked me, "Well, what about your feller, Hezzie? Are you gonna tell him how this feller kissed you?" I said, "*Tell* him how? I'm gonna *show* him how!"

* * *

One of the old gossips up at Grinder's Switch was tellin' me she noticed two people sittin' mighty, mighty close together at my house last night. I told her it was me and my boyfriend Hezzie. We was sittin' there together and then I took Hezzie into the lovin' room. She said, "That's living." And I said, "Boy, are you tellin' me!"

* * *

The big news this week from Grinder's Switch was our annual excursion to Tullahoma to the swimmin' hole over there. We chartered a bus to take us. You should have seen the way I was squeezed in between four fellers. It was wonderful! And Uncle Nabob, he come along with us, and when we got there, I asked him where was Aunt Ambrosia. He said, "She missed the bus. I seen her just as the bus was pullin' out." And I said, "Well, didn't you tell the bus driver to stop?" And he said, "No. But I did manage to wave good-bye!"

But I wore a pretty daring bathing suit I thought. I took my old suit and cut the sleeves out clean off to the shoulders. It was awesome. But there was one girl there looked like she should have chosen a more conservative bathing suit. See, she don't have the kind of figure that adds up. Well, it adds up all right, but it leaves too much to carry!

And you should have seen the suit that Lizzy Tinkem had on. It was some suit. Not much at the bottom, less at the top, and nothin' in between!

Brother was having fun at the swimmin' party. All the little younguns love to watch Brother when he's swimmin' in the water. You see, he's the only person that they've ever seen that could float on his back and paddle with his ears!

* * *

One day I put a pretty dress on, and some folks said it wasn't long enough. But it'll be long enough before I get another. But that dress was twenty-five years old, it was, and sure enough, when I told my boyfriend Hezzie that the dress was twenty-five years old, he said, "Minnie, it looks pretty good for the shape it's on. Now I'm not tryin' to say nothin' mean about your figure. You just oughta treat your figure like it was in a battle!" I said to him, "Treat my figure like it was in a battle?" And he said, "Yeah. You oughta regroup and bring up reinforcements!"

Brother, he tried to console me. He said, "Minnie, don't you worry. Don't you worry at all. You know there's other things that attract men, like charm, or poise, or brains." I told Brother, "I ain't never yet caught a feller whistlin' at a girl's brains!"

* * *

Somebody once asked me if they heard right that I was gonna be a cover girl. I told them, "Yes, I am." I got the idea right after I heard a feller say, "If I had a face like Minnie Pearl, I'd cover it!"

* * *

Last night we had a Valentine's social at Grinder's Switch, and there was a girl there. She's been up there to Grinder's Switch before to a party, and she's pretty, and she's real, real popular with the fellers. And all of 'em was kinda shinin' around her, and I heard one of the fellers say to my feller, Hezzie, "Whooee! Ain't she got an hourglass figure!" And old Hezzie said, "Yeah, and don't she make every second count!"

Then they played a game and my brother kissed that pretty girl. I reckon it's the first girl that Brother ever kissed in his whole life. I asked him the next mornin', "How'd you like it, Brother?" And he said, "I don't know much about it, but it's my hobby from now on!"

Then I walked up to this girl that was there and she was acting real smart. She looked at me and said, "Minnie Pearl, looks like to me you've been puttin' on a little weight." I said, "What are you talking about? I just lost five pounds!" She says, "Well, turn around. I think I found it!"

* * *

A couple was celebratin' their fiftieth wedding anniversary with a reception. They were standin' in line greetin' their friends and about halfway through, she hauled off and hit him! He looked surprised and said, "What was that for?" She said, "For fifty years of bad sex!" He thought about that a minute and then hauled off and hit *her*. Now it was her turn to look surprised and she said, "What on earth was that for?" And he answered, "For knowing the difference!"

* * *

Two men attending a big city convention were having dinner together and talking about the hotels they were staying in. The one man remarked that he was staying at a hotel that had nightly turndown service. Being from the country, the other man asked what he meant. The first man said, "Every night when I proposition the maids, I get turned down!"

* * *

A single man who was an absolute fanatic about golf finally got married, and on his wedding night he confessed to his new bride, "Honey, maybe I should have told you sooner, but I'm an avid golfer and hope you won't be too upset if you don't see me too much on weekends." "No," she sweetly replied, "and as long as we're making confessions, you should know that I was a hooker." "Oh, that's nothing to worry about," he replied. "We can fix that by moving your right hand a little on the grip and dropping your left foot back."

* * *

The talk of the town was a pretty young gal who also happened to be especially well-endowed. One summer afternoon, she entered a boutique and asked the manager, "May I try on that swimsuit in the window?" The manager eyed her approvingly and said, "By all means! It's been a slow day and it oughta help business!"

* * *

There was a very lovely and shapely young lady who was trying to board a city bus. But her arms were filled with packages, and she was wearing a dress that was obviously too tight to allow her to step up onto the bus for which she had been waiting for over fifteen minutes.

A crowd had formed behind her that was trying to board the busy bus too and began pushing her from behind. So, in an attempt to loosen her dress to climb the steps, she reached back, without anyone noticing, and pulled down on the zipper at the back of her dress.

Much to her surprise, it didn't seem to help. So she reached back again and lowered the zipper a little further. Even still, it didn't help, and she was still stuck.

Just then, a young man behind her in the crowd picked her up and deposited her gently onto the bus. This only embarrassed her more to which she gasped, "What right do you have to pick me up like that? I don't even know you!"

"Well, Miss," the young man replied, smiling and tipping his hat, "after you pulled my zipper down the second time, I started to think we were pretty good friends!"

* * *

There was a boy and a girl out in the country on a late evening drive. Not long after, the car stopped. She said, "Well! I suppose you're gonna give me the 'run-out-of-gas' routine, right?" He said, "Nope! It's the 'here after' routine." She was a little puzzled, so she asked him, "The 'here after' routine? What's that?" He said, "If you're not here after what I'm here after, then you'll be here after I've gone back to town!"

* * *

The shop foreman was working on a wall partition when a woman walked up to him and asked what he was doing. He said, "I'm locating studs in the wall with this stud finder." After contemplating his answer, the woman, with a gleam in her eye, asked, "Is there any chance you would loan me that thing for the weekend?"

* * *

There were these three fellows who died at the same time and were waiting to be accepted into heaven. When Saint Peter met them at the Pearly Gates, he asked each of them how he had died. The first fellow said, "I had a bad heart attack." The second fellow said, "I was in a car accident." The third fellow said, "I died of 'seen us.'" Saint Peter said, "Don't you mean *sinus*?" "No," the man said. "I was out with a married woman and her husband seen us."

* * *

A young housewife had just survived a hectic summer vacation with her two young children and was elated when she finally got them off to school. She said to herself, "I'm going to take a nice bath and relax." She filled the tub, took off her clothes and just as she was going to get in the doorbell rang. "Who's there?" she asked. "Blind man," came the reply. Thinking that he couldn't see her, she answered the door in her birthday suit. When she opened the door, the man said, "Nice body, lady. Now why don't you tell me where you want these blinds hung."

* * *

A rather embarrassed young couple walked into the small town library. They walked up to the librarian's desk. The woman was at least seventy years old and hadn't been married or had a boyfriend since she was fifty. They explained that they were planning to get married in a couple of weeks and wondered if she might be able to point out any books on sex.

"Oh yes," she answered with a cute little wink. "I file all of these books personally, and you'll find what you're looking for over there on the ancient history shelves!"

* * *

A doctor had just finished checking over a "not-so-young" patient. "I can't seem to find a thing wrong with you, but I do recommend that you give up half your love life."

After a long pause and deep thought the patient replied, "Doc, which half do you suggest I give up? Thinking about it or talking about it?"

* * *

Three couples approached the Pearly Gates and asked permission from Saint Peter to enter. To the first husband he responded, "You may *not* enter heaven. All your life you've been obsessed with money. Why, you even married a woman named Penny!"

He then turned to the second husband and responded, "You may *not* enter heaven. All your life you've been obsessed with food. Why, you even married a woman named Candy."

Taking his wife gently by the hand and looking very sad, the third husband said, "Come on, Fanny, we might as well get out of here!"

* * *

An elderly lady went to her doctor and asked him for some birth control pills to help her sleep. He informed her they weren't for sleeping. The old woman got mad and demanded the pills, so, knowing they would do her no good, he finally gave her a thirty-day supply just to get rid of her. Thirty days later, she returned for more pills. Again, he told her the birth control pills wouldn't help her sleep. "Oh yes they do!" she insisted. "I give one to my teenage granddaughter every morning, and that night I sleep like a log!"

* * *

A foxy young city lady was driving through the countryside on a hot summer night when she came upon a lake. Since the lake appeared isolated, the young lady decided to go skinny dipping, subsequently removing all of her clothing and diving into the lake.

*Minnie Pearl and fellow
performers, the "Duke of
Paducah," and Smiley Burnett
take a moment to pose at the
old WSM Studios in Nashville.*

Courtesy of Les Leverett

When she emerged from her dive, she observed an old man in a battered hat, beard, and bib overalls standing on the lake's bank grinning from ear to ear and staring at her. She quickly swam to shore, picked up an old discarded washbasin and placed it over her private parts and angrily shouted at the old man, "I guess you know what I'm thinking, you old wolf!" "Yes, ma'am," the old man answered politely. "You're thinking that old dishpan has a bottom in it, but it don't!"

* * *

A young woman in the upper berth of the Pullman car on the northbound train managed to attract the attention of the man in the lower berth who was sound asleep. She asked, "Sir, will you get me a blanket? I'm cold."

The man asked, "Are you married?" to which she replied, "No, I'm not." "Well, how would you like to pretend you and I are married?" he inquired. She shyly replied, "Oh! I think that would be fun!" He said gruffly, "Good! Then go get your own blanket."

* * *

Having to go forty miles into town to go shopping, a rancher's daughter asked her father if a ranch hand could drive the horse and buggy to take her. The next day they got started, and halfway there they stopped at an inn for the night. There was only one room left, so the ranch hand said he could sleep on the floor. When they got to the room the girl said that he could sleep in the bed, and she would put a pillow between them.

The next morning they were on the road again when the girl's hat flew off and sailed over a fence. The ranch hand stopped the horse and said, "I'll get your hat for you." The sweet young thing said, "Never mind! If you couldn't get over that pillow last night you sure can't get over that fence this morning!"

* * *

When hearing rumors of possible disturbances at a nearby nudist colony, the sheriff sent his young deputy there to patrol the area. Later that day the deputy called in to report the situation.

"How are things going out there?" asked the Sheriff. "No problems, Sheriff," replied the deputy, "except my badge is killing me!"

* * *

A fellow was telling his friend about his wife. He said, "My wife is incredibly beautiful. She has a beautiful disposition. She's an angel!" His friend replied, "You're lucky. Mine's still alive."

5.
Ralph Emery Remembers Minnie

It was my time at Ralph Emery's *Nashville Now* television program on TNN that afforded me the opportunity to get to know Minnie. When he introduced her, Ralph would refer to Minnie as his "Friday night girlfriend." It was his program that gave birth to the "Let Minnie Steal Your Joke" segment. The show's producers, TNN management, and Minnie agreed that having country's favorite comedienne telling jokes from fans would be the equivalent of down home rapture! As Minnie and practically every comic performer would tell you, there are no new jokes. Just new ways to tell the old ones.

While sitting with Ralph at his Music City office, we listened to some old recordings and watched video tapes where, amongst other things, I heard Minnie reflect on the evolution of her signature "Howdee!" In her own words it started out as a simple, polite country greeting to the audience and evolved into a robust "Howdee!" when she started to hit the big time. One of Ralph's most vivid memories from the "...Steal Your Joke" segment on TNN is a funny, but startling, moment that I will also never forget, as I was there.

Minnie had received roses that were placed between her and Ralph on the small table used for the segment. They were long-stem reds in a clear vase with glass marbles inside. Well, if you've never been to a television taping you wouldn't know that it's the equivalent of traveling from the North Pole to the

Equator in a matter of minutes. Before the lights are turned on, the studio is usually a chilly sixty-plus degrees, but when you add a million watts of lighting to the equation, even Brother could have used the "old math" to figure out that the mercury rises faster than fever from the smallpox.

Midway through the segment, the vase could stand no more. The temperature of the glass changed so rapidly that the vase exploded in a large, watery crash all over the studio floor losing its marbles in the process! It was as if we were in the middle of a turkey shoot and someone yelled, "Pull!" I don't recall everything that happened after the incident, but I will attest that the show did go on and the banter was colorful.

Ralph did share his favorite Minnie Pearl story with me. It comes, of course, from Grinder's Switch. It just proves that even in the country you shouldn't mix politics and religion. Oh, and by the way, don't forget all of your schoolin' and practicin' of the appropriate lingo for the region.

There was a time when Uncle Nabob was runnin' for constable up there in Grinder's Switch. And him and Lem Perkins ain't never been good friends. In fact they've been bitter enemies ever since anyone can remember. And even though Lem was known to go around talkin' about Uncle Nabob, Uncle Nabob went up to him anyway and said, "I know we ain't never been good friends. I know that. But please vote for me. I need your vote!" Lem says, "I wouldn't vote for you if you was Saint Peter his-self!" Uncle Nabob says, "Listen. If I was Saint Peter you couldn't vote for me. You wouldn't be in my district!"

6.
Take Two Lawyers and Call Me in the Mornin'

Every town has professionals. Okay, those of you "fellers" who are still a couple of chapters back, catch up! I'm talking about doctors, lawyers, policemen, morticians, and politicians. Grinder's Switch is no exception when it comes to putting up with—or should I say, standing firmly behind—these noble trades. I guess the only difference is that in the country, the old joke would be told, "What do you call a thousand lawyers at the bottom of a *creek*?"

Now doctoring in the country can sometimes literally be defined by the phrase "practicing medicine." In fact, in some of the stories I've heard it sounds like a few are still reading the medical books. But country doctors don't have to worry about things like health insurance or government assistance programs. All they need to care about is a cure for the common coal miner. Old Doc Payne is Grinder's Switch's contribution to the American Medical Association, at least that's what I think. I'm not sure anyone knows definitively where he went to medical school. Maybe he got his degree by mail order from Sears and Roebuck, or maybe it was passed down from his pappy. You know carrying on a family trade is certainly a way of life at the Switch. All in all, the old Doc seems to be a kind and caring man. But I'd be wary nonetheless if you happened to pass through town and fall ill. You see, rumor has it that old Doc Payne thinks anesthesia is the name of a pretty girl that lives over in Shady Grove.

The country is also a place where the law of the land can be the law of the moment. For example, a shotgun wedding doesn't usually require a gun permit, and the wedding itself is usually caused by an extensive holding period by the groom-to-be. And if you're thinking of visiting Moonshine McGinny's after the reception, just remember even in the country you can be accused and convicted of driving under the influence if caught plowing your name in a neighbor's cornfield while driving an old International Harvester. But don't worry, I'm pretty sure that public dunking has been replaced on the law books with a lesser punishment by the clientele of the local donut den.

As for dying, I believe there's no truth in the rumor that the Switch's local mortician, Mark Graves, is also the town taxidermist. Truth is that he does genuinely good work on some of the wildlife that roams the dirt roads of Grinder's Switch, and he is rarely caught lying down on the job. I'm reminded that Minnie once told one of the town's old critters that he had to change his way of doing things, that their quiet little hamlet couldn't tolerate him chasing around after every pretty girl that he saw. And just to make a point, she told him he was no different than the rest of the fellows in town, to which the man protested loudly and said, "There's lots of men here that don't chase after pretty girls!" Minnie looked him square in the eye and said, "Yeah, that's right. And don't they look natural!"

A rave review of Mr. Graves handiwork, I'm sure!

✳ ✳ ✳

I had a date with a handsome young feller today and it cost me some money. He was my doctor. I told him I was sufferin' from loss of appetite, loss of sleep, and loss of weight. And he said, "How old are you?" I said, "Twenty-one." He said, "Sufferin' from loss of memory too, ain't you?"

Now this feller was a mighty fine doctor, but he couldn't see eye to eye with me. His diagnosis was wrong. He wanted to take my tonsils out and I wanted him to take me out!

* * *

Uncle Nabob and Aunt Ambrosia came into town to help me do a little shoppin' for Sister. So, we went into one of them department stores and there was a lady demonstratin' a kind of a dress that she was gonna try to sell Sister. Uncle Nabob was watchin' her and this lady says, "Now you see this combination. If you take off the bolero, you have a play suit! And you take off part of this bodice here, then you've got a sunsuit! And you take off this skirt, and you've got a bathing suit!" And Uncle Nabob said, "Yeah, and if you take off any more then you got a lawsuit!"

* * *

I was talkin' to one of my friends back home tellin' 'em about my bein' hit on the head. I got a blow on my head so I think I'm gonna go see one of them, psychi...see-chree..., one of them head doctors. He told me, "You don't want to go to one of them fellas!" I asked why not. He said, "I went one time and all he told me was that I was melancholy. I had a head like a melon and a face like a collie!"

* * *

Old Link Shank's wife, up there at Grinder's Switch, had a peculiar thing happen to her this past week. She went in town and told old Doc Payne about it; he's the doctor up there. She went over there and said, "Doc, I've got to do somethin' about Link. He's got to where he thinks he's a refrigerator." And Doc Payne said, "Well now, Mancy, don't you worry about that now. He'll get over thinking that he's a refrigerator." She said, "I know that. But you see, he sleeps with his mouth wide open and that little old light inside keeps me awake all night!"

* * *

This winter I'm going to learn my hula-hula dances. I've got to practice my hula dancing 'cause last winter I got a slight cold, and I went to old Doc Payne. He told me I should "do everything I could to try to shake it off!"

* * *

Nelly Stern had a birthday party this week. Ain't it awful how old some folks get! I remember when me and Nelly was the same age. Now she's got younguns my age!

Brother was at the party, and ever since the New Year he's been tryin' to make a fresh start. He always gets his face slapped. And Uncle Nabob was sure havin' a good time. He don't ever do nothin' by halves. Just by fifths.

Nelly Stern's niece was there from the city, and she had on one of them low-neck, low-back evening dresses. She sure was a live wire! She sparked with the men, shocked the women, and wasn't properly insulated!

We made a big discovery at that party about Mark Graves, our local undertaker. We found out somethin' about him that we didn't know. He's a real good musician. He can play two instruments at the same time. Out of one side of his mouth he plays the trumpet, and out of the other side of his mouth he plays the clarinet. Yes sir. The other night out of the left side of his mouth he was playin' "Life Is Just a Bowl of Cherries," and out of the right side of his mouth he played "Under the Shade of the Old Apple Tree." And all the time he was playin', he was blowin' seeds out of the middle of his mouth!

* * *

I'm mighty proud to know that folks think of me as a good, clean American girl. I know they think I'm clean on account of I just heard one feller say to another feller, "That dame sure looked washed out!" Well now, maybe I look washed out, but I ain't washed *up!*

It wasn't so long ago I had a chance to marry a feller with fifty thousand dollars. But I couldn't raise the fifty thousand dollars. Then there's the time I could have married an X-ray specialist. He took pictures of me after I swallowed a diamond ring. He was the only feller that could ever see anything in me!

* * *

One day a man was riding his bicycle down the main highway and the chain broke. He couldn't fix it, so he starting pushing it until a man in a brand new black Corvette stopped to ask if he could help. He said he had a rope they could tie to the bicycle and the car and pull the cyclist to the next town. They agreed and decided that if the Corvette got too fast, the man on the bicycle would honk his horn to slow him down. So they set off down the road.

Just then a man in a flashy red Corvette drove alongside the black Corvette and challenged the man to a race. So off they sped, apparently forgetting the man on the bicycle who was frantically honking his horn! Finally the sheriff caught up with the two speedy Corvettes and the bicycle. The sheriff routinely called in for a backup and when the station asked why he couldn't handle it himself he said, "Well, I know what to do with the two Corvettes who were doing 120 miles an hour, but what should I do with the guy on the bike who was honking his horn to pass them?"

* * *

It seems the government was trying to get ol' Chief Runamoc to move his teepee. Well, the Chief objected because his family had lived on that same land for generations, and so he wanted to see a lawyer right away. The government agent told him, "Go down the street and take a left to the lawyer's office." But instead of a left, Chief took a right and walked into the doctor's office by mistake. The doctor said, "What seems to be your problem, Chief?" Chief said, "Chief no move!" The doctor nodded and said, "I see. That's not a problem. Just take this bottle of medicine and come back in two days." So after two days the chief went back and the doctor asked him, "Well, did you move?" Chief said, "Chief had to move. Teepee full!"

* * *

A man took his wife to a psychiatrist. After waiting for about an hour, the nurse said to them, "The doctor will see you now."

Ernest Tubb looks on as Minnie and her favorite straight man, Rod Brasfield laugh through one of their regular routines.

Courtesy of Les Leverett

The doctor asked, "May I help you?" The man said, "Doc, it's not me, it's my wife. She thinks she's a lawn mower." The doctor asked, "How long has this gone on?" He replied, "Oh, for about a year now."

Surprised, the doctor asked, "Well, why didn't you bring her in here sooner?" The man replied, "I couldn't! The last guy that borrowed her didn't return her for six months!"

* * *

This man had not been feeling well so he went to a doctor. After the doctor checked him over, he told him that he was very sick and didn't have long to live. So, the man asked the doctor what he suggested that he should do with the time he had left. The doctor answered, "You should buy an old worn-out station wagon, find the ugliest and meanest woman you can with six or seven mean kids, marry her, and all take a trip to Mexico in the car."

The man replied, "But doctor, how is that going to make me live longer?" The doctor answered, "I didn't say it would make you live longer, but it sure will make it *seem* like you have!"

✳ ✳ ✳

Old Mister Johnson sat down at the doctor's desk. "What's your problem?" asked the doctor. "Well, Doc, after the first, I'm very tired. After the second, I feel all in. After the third, my heart begins to pound. After the fourth, I break out in a cold sweat, and after the fifth, I'm so exhausted I feel I could die!" "Incredible!" said the doctor. "How old are you?" "Eighty-five," replied the old man. "Well, at eighty-five why don't you stop after the first?" the doctor asked. "But Doctor, how can I stop at the first when I live on the fifth?"

✳ ✳ ✳

Two carpenters were working and one was up above the other one. Suddenly, he dropped his saw and it fell down and hit the man below and cut off his ear!

So they rushed him to the hospital with the ear so they could sew it back on. When the man saw the ear he said, "That's not my ear!" "Yes it is," the doctor said. He then asked, "Why don't you think it's your ear?" The man said, "'Cause mine had a pencil behind it!"

✳ ✳ ✳

Two men walked into the doctor's office in a rural community and one man was limping. The older man said, "Doc, fix up my son-in-law's leg. He's limpin' real bad since I shot him yesterday!"

The doctor said, "Zeke, you should be ashamed of yourself for shooting your son-in-law like that." Zeke replied, "Well Doc, he wasn't my son-in-law when I shot him!"

✳ ✳ ✳

A sheriff spotted a car parked along the road near the creek so he pulled over to check it out. As he peeked through the bushes, he saw a young lady skinny dipping and said, "Hey there, young lady, you aren't allowed to swim in this creek." The pretty young girl stood up and said, "Well, why didn't you tell me that before I took all of my clothes off?" The sheriff said, "There isn't any law against folks takin' their clothes off."

* * *

A pediatrician in town always plays a game with some of his young patients to test their knowledge of body parts. One day, while pointing to a little boy's ear, the doctor asked him, "Is this your nose?" Immediately the little boy turned to his mother and said, "Mom, I think we'd better find a new doctor!"

* * *

A driver was talking to his friend and missed stopping for a red light. He was halfway across the busy intersection when a police whistle brought him to his senses and pulled him over. The man explained, "Officer, I tried to stop and couldn't. I think there is something wrong with my car." "You're right," the cop answered, "I think it's the nut that holds the steering wheel."

* * *

A highway patrolman saw a man speeding down the interstate. The patrolman gave chase, turning on his blue light. The man sped up, so the patrolman turned on his siren. When the man finally gave up and stopped, the patrolman last week asked, "Didn't you see my blue light?" The man said, "Yes." "Didn't you hear my siren?" "Yes." "Well, why didn't you stop?" asked the patrolman. "Well, my wife ran off with a patrolman and I thought it was you, and you were bringing her back!"

7.
Bill Anderson
Remembers Minnie

"Whispering" Bill Anderson is one of the most popular legends of the Grand Ole Opry and country music in general. But, like almost anyone you talk to from the biggest to the youngest stars, they all speak humbly and respectfully about the Queen of Country Comedy. "You know, Minnie Pearl was one of those people that I don't remember meeting for the first time because I felt like I always knew her," Bill told me backstage. He also said he didn't remember when she wasn't a part of his life, "first as a fan, of course as a co-worker on the Opry, and then later on as a friend."

Bill mentioned that he may have told this story in one of his own books, but it's his favorite memory and worth telling again. It happened while standing backstage at one of the last road shows Minnie Pearl ever did. It took place in Charlotte, North Carolina. Minnie, Bill, Johnny Russell, and Little Jimmy Dickens were touring together, and Minnie was in the wings getting ready to go on. "I walked up and just kinda put my arm around her as we were prone to do after she had the bout with cancer," Bill reflected. "And every time she would see you she'd say, 'I love you.' And you'd say, 'I love you Minnie.' It broke down a lot of barriers."

In this instance while they were standing there talking, Minnie looked up at Bill ("and this was Minnie Pearl!" he said in an almost stunned awe) and she said, "Do you reckon there'll ever come a time when we won't be nervous before we go on stage?" Bill replied, "Minnie Pearl, are you standing there telling me that you're nervous?" She answered, "Yes, I've got butterflies." But she continued with words that Bill confessed he has carried with him ever since, and that he holds dear every time he gets a little flutter before taking the stage. She said, "If you don't get a few butterflies before you go on the stage, then it doesn't mean as much to you as it should." "God love you, Minnie," Bill said with deep admiration. "What a beautiful thing for her to say, and what an *amazing* thing for her to say."

Bill grinned as he remembered Minnie's incredible sense of timing, especially when she worked with Roy Acuff. One of his favorite routines that she and the "King of the Opry" used to perform was as short and simple as they come.

> "Minnie, tell me about the lady in Grinder's Switch with all the children," Roy would say. Minnie would answer, "Oh, you mean the lady who had so many children she ran out of names—(long pause)—to call her husband!"

Still smiling, Bill confessed that Roy and Minnie were a magical combination. If you look back in time at the most celebrated comedic teams, they were the ones that made it seem like they weren't working at all. Roy and Minnie were that great. Each knowing exactly how to complement the other's performance. "Minnie didn't need a straight man," Bill said. But her teamwork with Roy made even the simplest joke seem better, like this favorite of Bill's about Brother, back in Grinder's Switch.

> "You know a lot of people don't think much of what Brother's done with his life back in Grinder's Switch. You know, it's not that he's a failure. He just started at the bottom and he likes it there!"

8.
Pass the Plate, But Hold the Cornbread

While this seems to be a time when virtue could be mistaken for a new brand of perfume and integrity confused with a brand of car, people at the Switch are well known for their strong moral fiber. Now Grinder's Switch may not be considered to be directly along the Bible Belt, but I do think someone merely missed a loop and the town's just waiting for a rethread of its holy britches.

It's a country town where people live the good, clean life expecting their reward to be waiting at the Pearly Gates with Saint Peter and a place where foul words have only to do with baseball and chicken coops. It's a place where cheating on your spouse means sneaking an extra piece of homemade apple pie from the cold cellar in the middle of the night. It's a town where family values mean buying the jumbo slab of ground beef on sale at the Piggly Wiggly. And be warned that if you don't live by this strict set of rules, you can surely expect to toil in heat, sweat, and agony when you go in a blaze of disgrace straight to *heck*! (In a handbag, of course.)

In spite of everything I've just told you, it seems that folks in the Switch are no more perfect than anyone else, they just have a clearer understanding of how other people sin. Even though there aren't a lot of glass houses in the country, a little mud slinging is known to happen. But let's leave the preaching up to those who have actually received the proper calling.

* * *

There's this lady from Grinder's Switch who's a hundred and four years old. Her mammy and pappy said they was afraid they'd never raise that youngun! Even though she don't look like she's gonna need it any time soon, she's got her funeral all fixed up. She went to the preacher the other day and said she wanted to have her funeral all ready. She said she wanted to have nothin' but women pall bearers. When the preacher asked her why, she said, "Them men wouldn't take me out when I was alive, so I don't want 'em takin' me out after I'm dead!"

* * *

There was a poor young man who had an accident and fell into a deep coma and was feared to soon be dead. But suddenly, he started to make a remarkable recovery and was able to receive his friends. One of them asked what it felt like to be practically dead. "Dead?" he said to his friend. "Well, I never really worried. I knew I wasn't dead because my feet were cold and I was hungry." His friend asked him, "Well, how would that make you so sure you weren't dead?" The young man said, "Well, I knew that if I was in heaven, I wouldn't be hungry! And if I were in the other place, my feet definitely wouldn't be cold!"

* * *

There were five people flying on a private plane that had suddenly developed severe engine trouble and was going to crash. Unfortunately, there were only four parachutes and on board was the pilot, the President of the United States, a Harvard scholar with the highest IQ in the world, a priest, and a young hippie. Knowing their fate, the pilot grabbed one chute and bailed out immediately. The President said, "Well, I have to run the most powerful country in the world," so he grabbed a chute and bailed out next. The Harvard scholar said, "Since I'm the smartest man in the world, I need to continue to teach people," so he grabbed a chute and bailed out next. This left just the priest and the hippie. The priest looked at the hippie and said, "Son, I am saved and ready to die, and since there is just one more chute, you take it and jump." The young man just smiled and said, "No, Father, we have two chutes left. The smartest man in the world just grabbed my backpack and jumped."

* * *

Two men named Bill Smith lived near one another. In fact, they lived in the same neighborhood. One was a preacher, and the other a businessman. The preacher died in August at about the same time the other man went to Florida on business. When the other Bill arrived in Florida, he sent his wife a telegram telling her of his safe arrival. But the message was accidentally delivered to the wife of the recently deceased preacher. You know what the telegram said? It said, "Arrived safely... but boy is it hot here!"

* * *

A woman who faithfully played the lottery finally won twenty million dollars! But she was afraid to tell her husband for fear that he would drop over dead of a heart attack. So she went to her neighbor and asked for a suggestion as to how to tell him. Her neighbor told her she had no idea. So the woman went to her minister and asked his advice. The minister said, "Don't worry about it. I'll just take him to lunch and I'll find a way to break it to him gently." So the minister asked the woman's husband to lunch and while they were eating he said to the man, "Boy! A lot of people are winning the lottery these days. What would you do if you won that big twenty-million-dollar jackpot?" The man replied, "Well, first, I'd give half to you and the church," whereupon the minister dropped over dead of a heart attack.

* * *

If you've never seen a river baptism you've missed half your life. One day with the whole congregation watching, the old

Not commonly recognized for her singing talents, Minnie Pearl loved to play the piano and sing as seen here in her early days on the road.

Courtesy of Les Leverett

preacher who was a little hard of hearing dunked an old lady down in the water, baptized her, and brought her up. As he did it, he asked her, "Do you believe?" She was choking and could barely get out the words so he put her under again and said, "Do you believe?" She was still waterlogged and barely whispered the words, so he put her under again and said, "Do you believe?" Finally, she gasped for air and yelled, "Yes! I believe!"

With that the preacher said, "Then go out on the hill and tell them you believe!" When she came running up the hill she yelled out, "I believe that old fool was trying to drown me!"

* * *

Three preachers went out one day on a fishing trip to a big lake. After catching several nice ones, a violent thunderstorm suddenly erupted and the three were stranded out in the middle of the lake being tossed violently about in their boat. "Brothers," said one of the preachers, "it doesn't look like we're going to make it back to shore. This may very well be the end. So I'll say right now we should confess our most awful sins."

The first preacher replied, "Well, I like to look at pretty women." The second preacher said, "Well, I like to sip a little whiskey every now and then." The two then turned to the third preacher for his reply and right at that very moment the skies cleared, the wind and rain stopped, and the storm surprisingly ended. He said, "Well, I confess that I love to gossip and can't wait to get back to town!"

*** * *

The Sunday school lesson this week was about Noah's ark, and the teacher asked the children what they thought Noah might have done to kill time for those forty long and dreary days. One little boy said, "I bet he spent a lotta time fishing!" Another little boy said, "He couldn't have done that. He only had two worms!"

*** * *

In church one Sunday morning, a little boy pulled out his cap pistol and fired it during the sermon. His mother yanked him to his feet and marched him outside intending to punish him then and there!

A little old lady followed them both out saying, "Don't spank that boy. He scared the Devil out of more people today than the preacher has in ten years!"

*** * *

A minister who was walking along a road saw a crowd of boys surrounding a dog. "What are you doing with that dog?" asked the kindly minister. One boy spoke up and said, "Whoever tells the biggest lie wins the dog." "Oh, my!" exclaimed the minister. "When I was a boy like you, I never told a lie."

There was a moment's silence until one of the little fellows said, "Here. You win the dog."

* * *

Sam died and went to heaven. Saint Peter met him at the Pearly Gates and said, "I'm sorry, Sam, but we are filled to capacity. I can't let you in." Sam said, "What do you mean you can't let me in? I've gotta get in! Isn't there any way?" Saint Peter said, "The only way I can let you in is if you know God's name." Sam thought for a minute and then replied, "It's Andy." Saint Peter said, "Why in the world would you think his name is Andy?" Sam replied, "It's in that song that we sing at church. You know, the one that goes, 'Andy walks with me, Andy talks with me'!"

* * *

While visiting his parishioners one Saturday afternoon, a pastor knocked on the door of a church member but got no response. He was quite annoyed because he could hear footsteps and knew that the mother of the family must be there. Leaving his calling card, the minister wrote the following: Revelation 3:20 - "Behold, I stand at the door and knock: If any man hear my voice and open the door, I will come in to him."

That Sunday as the parishioners filed out of church after the service, the woman who had refused to answer the door greeted the pastor and handed him her card with Genesis 3:10 written on it. Later, the minister looked it up and it read: "I heard thy voice in the garden, and I was afraid, because I was naked; and I hid myself."

* * *

After the bride returned from her honeymoon she came crying home to her mother. "Living with Bill is going to be horrible," she wailed. "He's an atheist and doesn't believe there's a place called hell." Her mother said, "Don't worry, honey. Between you and me, we'll have no trouble showing him how wrong he is!"

* * *

After delivering an outrageously long, ridiculous funeral sermon about a crazy man who had passed on, the preacher peered into the open casket and said, "What we have before us is only the shell. God has already taken the nut away."

* * *

Two American ministers traveling in Germany decided to go to church. Speaking no German, they decided to play it safe by doing whatever the dignified looking gentleman in front of them did. During the service, the pastor made a special announcement and the man in front of them arose. The two Americans stood up quickly only to be met with roars of laughter.

After the service, they found that the pastor spoke English. "What was so funny?" asked one of the ministers. The pastor replied, "I was announcing a baptism and asked the father of the child to stand."

* * *

A preacher was discussing with his wife what he would preach on Sunday. He decided on skiing. His wife laughed, "Skiing? What kind of sermon is that? You don't even know anything about it." But come Sunday the preacher stood up behind the pulpit ready to start the skiing message when he suddenly saw a boy and girl kissing on the back row. So thinking quickly, he changed the message to sex.

His wife didn't make it to church that Sunday, but the following day a lady from church called her and said, "That was the best sermon your husband has preached in a while. It was really truthful." The preacher's wife exclaimed, "I don't know how. He's only tried it twice. Once before we were married and once after."

* * *

A group of students at the seminary were going door to door selling Bibles to raise money for the school. As they weren't having too much luck, another student, who had a speech impediment, asked the headmaster if he could try to sell some. The headmaster said, "Bless you for asking, but I'm not sure you can sell Bibles with your speech impediment." He said "Ju-ju-just let me t-t-tr-tr-try."

The student set off on his quest and when he returned he had outsold all of the others combined! The headmaster was amazed and said, "Tell me your secret! How did you sell more Bibles than all of the other guys?" The student replied, "Well, I a-a-as-asked them if they w-w-wa-wa-wanted to b-b-bu-bu-buy a B-B-Bi-Bi-Bible or did they w-w-wa-wa-want me to r-re-read it to them!"

* * *

A preacher who looked like Conway Twitty rang the doorbell of an old lady's house. When she answered the door, she said, "Conway Twitty!" The preacher said, "No, I'm Reverend Jones, and I'm holding a revival meeting at the little church on the corner. Sure would like for you to attend the service."

He then went to the next house. A middle-aged woman came to the door. She screamed, "Conway Twitty!" He explained the same thing to her and invited her to attend the service at the church.

He then went to the last house on the block, rang the doorbell, and a pretty young woman who had just gotten out of the bathtub answered the door with only a towel draped around her. When she saw him she threw out her arms and the towel fell to the floor as she screamed, "Conway Twitty!" To which the reverend replied, "Hello, Darlin'."

* * *

While traveling, two nuns ran out of gas and proceeded to walk to the nearest gas station. Upon arriving there, they were told by the attendant that he didn't have a container that they could carry gasoline back to their car with. He suggested they look through a scrap pile in the rear of the station. So after sorting through the pile, one sister found a bedpan with a long spout and they decided that it would be a good thing to use. After pumping some gas into it, they returned to the car and as they were pouring the gas in the tank two priests drove by. One priest remarked to the other, "I have to confess. Those nuns have a lot more faith than I do!"

* * *

Last Sunday at church, after the sermon, the offering plate was being passed around when a wife whispered to her husband, "Honey, your fly is open." Not understanding her he said, "What?" She repeated, "Your fly is open." Just then the offering plate went by and he zipped it up.

At home after church one of their daughters told her mom that she had seen what had happened and said, "I always wondered where Dad kept his billfold!"

* * *

A little boy rushed home from Sunday school and ran in to his mother and said, "Mommy! Mommy! Did you know that they had Honda cars back in the Bible days!" His mother looked at him puzzled and said, "Why son, that can't be. Where did you hear such a thing?" And her son replied, "Well, our Sunday school teacher said that one of those guys in the Bible said "when we go we'll all go in one Accord."

* * *

When asked to say the family prayer, a young child took the opportunity to list, loud and clear, the toys he wanted for his birthday.

His father told him, "You don't need to be so loud! The heavenly Father can hear you even if you whisper."

The child replied, "Yeah, but Grandpa can't!"

* * *

The local preacher was talking to four or five little boys. He asked them, "How many of you want to go to heaven?" They all held up their hands except for one. The preacher asked,

"Tommy, what's wrong? Don't you want to go to heaven?" Little Tommy said, "Yes! Of course I do! But I thought you were getting up a load to go right now!"

* * *

One Sunday, while the preacher was preaching his usual long and laborious sermon, Brother and Sister Jones were sitting in the front pew when Brother Jones fell fast asleep and started snoring. The preacher stopped and said to Sister Jones, "Would you please wake Brother Jones! He's disturbing the whole church with his snoring!" Sister Jones replied, "No way! You put him to sleep so you wake him up!"

* * *

A saloon keeper sold his old tavern to the local church. The enthusiastic church members tore out the bar, added some new lighting, gave the whole place a fresh coat of paint, and installed some pews. Unbeknownst to anyone, a parrot that belonged to the saloon keeper was left behind.

During the first Sunday service, the bird was watching from the rafters. When the minister appeared, the bird squawked, "New proprietor!" When the men who led the worship marched in, the bird again squawked and said, "New floor show!" But when the congregation stood to start the worship service, the bird turned and looked at them and said, "Same old crowd!"

* * *

The local preacher and his wife were visiting the home of a member of their congregation and were invited to stay for dinner. At the dinner table the proud mother asked her five-year-old son to say grace. The boy said, "Mom, I don't know what to say." The mother said, "Just say what you hear your Daddy say all the time." The little boy bowed his head and said, "Good God! Where does all the money go?"

* * *

An older couple was sitting in church holding hands. When the service was over, a lady who had been sitting behind them leaned over and said, "It sure does make me happy to see people who have been married as long as you have still so much in love that you want to hold hands." The wife looked at the woman and said, "Love has nothing to do with it. I was trying to keep him from cracking his knuckles."

* * *

Courtesy of Les Leverett

Cousin Minnie Pearl could be somewhat mischievous and a little bit playful, but she was always a country lady who throughout her career on stage and screen brought laughter to audiences of all ages.

The town church was holding its revival, and different families would invite the preacher to dinner each night. On one night the minister didn't know how to get to the family's house, so the dad said, "We'll let our son ride with you and show you the way." On the way the son said, "I bet you don't know what we're having for dinner!" The preacher said, "I'll bet it's chicken."

The boy said, "Nope. It's buzzard!" The preacher said, "How do you know?" The boy said, "I heard my mama and daddy talking this morning and they said, 'We gotta have the old buzzard for dinner one day so it might as well be today!'"

* * *

A priest was preparing the Eulogy for a well-known citizen of their town when he was approached by Paul, the brother of the deceased, who said, "I know my brother John's reputation wasn't sterling, so would it be possible for him to go out as a saint? I'll give the church ten thousand dollars if you'll put that in your eulogy."

The priest, who realized that his parish could really use the money, wanted to make sure he understood exactly what Paul wanted him to do. "You mean, all I have to do is say the words 'John was a saint' and you'll give me the money?" Paul said, "Yep!" So, the two agreed and the priest thanked Paul for his generosity.

At the funeral, the priest began his eulogy in his usual manner by saying, "We are gathered here to pay our last respects to John. Poor John. He was selfish, he had a terrible temper, he beat his wife, not to mention that he was unfaithful, and he was known to do a lot of gambling." He paused for a moment, remembering the ten thousand dollars and then said, "Now if you think the sins of poor John were many, compared to his living brother Paul, I must say, that poor 'John was a saint!'"

9.
Johnny Russell Remembers Minnie

Johnny Russell has always entertained the Opry crowd with a good story or a quick joke, or both. Naturally, this comes along with some of the many hit songs he has written and/or recorded over the years. Most would agree that he's as comfortable as a comedian or singer onstage, and I've seen him hold an audience in either role.

When I spoke to Johnny, he was very quick to deliver his favorite Minnie Pearl joke. It was a story that I'm sure I borrowed from her, too, as I regularly included it in my audience warm-up routine. Like Johnny said that evening, "If it's a good joke, it doesn't have to take a long time to tell it!" Sorry, Johnny. Having told this one so many times myself, I embellished just a little!

There was a little boy who was acting up terribly. His mother warned him that if he didn't stop, she was gonna have to give him a whippin'! Well, he kept on misbehaving until his mom finally said, "That's it!" and she proceeded to give him the spanking of his life. The little boy went crying all the way upstairs, ran into his mom's bedroom, stood in front of her full-length mirror, and dropped his britches. He took one look and went, "Hmph!" Then he marched straight back downstairs to his mom and said, "Boy, I sure hope you're happy! You cracked it!"

10.
Younguns, and Plenty of 'Em

People out in Grinder's Switch don't have children. No, it isn't a scientific problem. People at the Switch have what you call in the country, "younguns." Those are the products of the careful affiliations between the mockingbirds and honeybees of the Tennessee hills. However, one thing that seems to be quite common there is that having enough younguns never seems to be the problem. In fact, it's quite the opposite! I think that Ponce de Leon was barking up the wrong scrub pine when he was looking for the fountain of youth in the Sunshine State. If he had just come to Grinder's Switch he would have at least found what could have been called "the gurgling spring of younguns!" I think there really is something to that saying, "It's in the water."

But, I guess it's just a natural thing to want to have built-in company if you're ever feeling lonely and it's too late to drive to town. By just hollering out as many names as you can remember off the top of your head, you can have a full-blown social event if all the younguns are at home. When you hear tales of the characters at the Switch and out in the country, it's almost hard to believe that the stork has done a flyby so many times considering how many old buzzards are on patrol out there.

The other thing about younguns is that there's an incredibly frightening period in their lives when they know and tell nothing but the truth. Pardon me while I jump into the modern era for a second, but I have to admit that I think kids were the original, recordable Walkman tape recorders. What I mean is that if you say something out loud you can be sure it will be repeated word for word at the most inopportune time. Well, it's no different at the Switch, except *there* recording tape is the roll of paper a stenographer uses at the courthouse.

Now when a ladies' social group gets together, you can be sure that the overwhelming cackle from the henhouse is that younguns are definitely and categorically cute—well, to a point at least. However, when the menfolk get together to talk about their younguns, they use words like strappin', handsome, and hireable. And if a man has a son, then it becomes his absolute mission in life to impart upon that youngun the secrets of the toolshed. "Why son, the toolshed is a mystic place. Sometimes it's a place for tools. Sometimes it's a place for a whippin'. Sometimes it's a place for a little hanky-panky. And sometimes its a place to sack for the evening if Mammy finds out who you've been hanky-pankying with!"

Ah! With age comes wisdom. All I can say is that if I ever have younguns, I hope they don't become wise men.

✱ ✱ ✱

Up in Grinder's Switch, the Orson Tugwells had their annual and yearly visit from the stork. That makes fifteen. Somebody said to me, "She's had fifteen children altogether?" I told 'em, "Well, not all together. One at a time!"

Uncle Nabob says they must be stork ravin' crazy by now! They've been given the bird so many times. I told Miss Tugwell she oughta be like Lath Plodgett's wife. She named her children Eenie, Meenie, Minee, and Charlie. Miss Tugwell said, "Well, what happened to Mo?" I told her, "She said there ain't gonna be no Mo!"

✱ ✱ ✱

I'm telling you it ain't easy these days for a young, pretty, attractive girl to save her kisses for the man she loves. Some fella's always popping up wantin' to close out the account.

But I don't have to worry none about fellers as long as I've got my feller, Hezzie. I keep tellin' Hezzie that there ain't nothin' like wedded bliss. Hezzie says, "I ain't denying that there's nothin' like married bliss, that is if you don't raise too many little blisters!"

* * *

One time Aunt Ambrosia went for a three-month visit to her sister's. To keep Uncle Nabob out of trouble while she was gone, she gave him somethin' to mend. Someone asked me, "Was it a sweater or some socks?" I told her, "No, a broken leg!"

You might think Uncle Nabob's got trouble, but there's a feller down in Grinder's Switch named Mr. Sedge Poodree, and he runs a big farm down there near the switch. He's got eight younguns, all girls. Now, it certainly would be kind of nice runnin' the farm if he had four or five boys to help him. Of course now, you take eight girls, and they can do a lot of things, too. Last week, one of them government agents came through makin' a survey, and he went to Mr. Poodree and said, "In running this big farm, Mr. Poodree, what do you consider your biggest problem? Boll weevils? Crows?" He said, "No. Travelin' salesmen."

* * *

A little boy up in Grinder's Switch asked me to settle an argument once. He asked me, "What color are buttercups?" I told him, "Well, everybody knows that buttercups are yellow." He said, "Well, if buttercups are yellow, what color are hiccups?" I told him, "Burple."

* * *

A little boy who lived in the country was asked by his elderly aunt to go down to the spring and fetch her a pail of water.

The little boy obeyed and went down to the spring. When he started to dip the pail in the water, he saw a mean looking pair of eyes staring straight back at him. He jumped up and ran hurriedly back to the house.

"Where's my water?" his aunt asked. He said, "I couldn't get you no water 'cause there's a big ol' alligator in that spring!"

His aunt laughed and replied, "That old alligator has been living down there for years. He's probably just as afraid of you as you are of him!" The little boy replied, "Well, if he's just as scared as me, then that water ain't fit to drink!"

* * *

A boy was filling out his college questionnaire to help determine a compatible roommate. Beside the questions, "Do you make your bed regularly?" and "Do you consider yourself a neat person?" he checked the boxes marked "Yes."

His mom, who had been reading over his shoulder and knowing better of him, asked him why he had lied.

He answered, "Well, if I tell the truth they're liable to stick me in with some slob!"

* * *

A little girl was given a watch and a bottle of perfume as birthday gifts. She kept pestering people, "See my watch? Smell my perfume?" A little later on her mother said, "Dear, the minister is coming for supper and I don't want you to bother him about your watch and perfume."

So the little girl obeyed her mother. But while they were sitting at the table she just couldn't take it anymore, so she said to the minister, "I'm not supposed to talk about this, but anything you hear, and anything you smell, it's me!"

* * *

Back in town there's a store with a sign in the front window that says, "Cards for every occasion." Inside, a little boy had been poring over the stock of cards for some time when a clerk finally asked, "Just what is it you're looking for, sonny? We've got cards for every occasion. Do you need birthday greetings? A message to a sick friend? Anniversary congratulations to your ma and pa?"

The little boy shook his head and replied, "No. Have you got anything in the line of blank report cards?"

* * *

A five-year-old was watching his mother change the baby.
When she overlooked sprinkling the tot's backside with tal-
cum powder and hurried him into his diaper, the five-year-
old reproved her sharply and said, "Hey Mom, you forgot to
salt him!"

* * *

After attending the weekly church service, a woman who was
always critical was talking to her neighbor. She complained
that the seats were too hard, the singing was off key, and the
preaching was poor. At that point her little girl who had
gone with her spoke up. "But Mama, what did you expect for
only a dime?"

* * *

A little boy was told by his teacher, "You're going to have to
stop speaking out in the classroom or I'll have to punish you."
The little boy said, "I know, teacher, but I just can't help it. You
see, my father was a preacher, and my mother is a woman."

* * *

A grandchild went to his grandfather and asked him if he
could make a noise like a frog. His grandpa said, "Why do you
want me to do that?"
    He replied, "Well, Mom and Dad said when you croak we're
goin' to Disney World!"

* * *

A little boy was misbehaving at school one day and the
teacher caught him. She said, "Didn't I promise you that I'd
punish you if I caught you misbehaving again?"
    "Yes," said the boy. "But since I broke *my* promise, I
thought you might as well break yours!"

* * *

A grandma gave each of her two small granddaughters a heart-shaped sachet on Valentine's Day. She told them it was something they should put in their drawers so they would smell good.

The granddaughters examined and smelled them for quite some time, and then the older of the two quietly said, "Grandma, do we wear 'em in the front or in the back?"

* * *

The young daughter of divorced parents had spent the weekend with her dad and was reporting to her mother what had happened. "Daddy had a strange woman in his apartment over the weekend," she said. Her mother was very upset about this and said, "I can't believe he had the nerve to put you in such a filthy, disgusting environment!" The daughter said, "I know. That's exactly what the strange woman said, too. And she also told him she didn't do windows!"

* * *

Three young boys were arguing over whose dad was the fastest. The first boy said, "My dad drives a drag racing car and goes three hundred miles an hour, so I say he's the fastest!" The second boy bragged, "That's nothing! My dad's a fighter jet pilot and flies faster than the sound barrier, so I say he's the fastest."

The third boy just laughed and said, "My dad's got you all beat. He works for the government and his job doesn't get out until five-thirty but he's home by three o'clock every day!"

* * *

A grandpa and his grandson were building a tree house out of old, dry lumber, and every time they hit a board with a hammer the knots fell out. The grandson said, "What are the holes for, Grandpa?" His grandpa said, "Them are knotholes, boy!" The grandson said, "Well, if they're not holes, what are they?"

Even the finest performers rehearse as seen here when Archie Campbell, Tennessee Ernie Ford, and Minnie Pearl run through their number before a television appearance.

Courtesy of Les Leverett

* * *

One day a father went up to his young son and said, "Son, somebody knocked over the outhouse. Did you do it?" "No sir, I did not," he replied. "Now Son, I'll give you one more chance to tell me the truth. Did you knock over the outhouse?" Again, the little boy denied it.

So the father decided to tell his son the story of George Washington chopping down the cherry tree. He continued, "When George Washington's father asked him if he chopped down the cherry tree, George said, 'Daddy, I cannot tell a lie. I chopped down the cherry tree.' And because George told the truth, he did not get a whippin'. Now, for the last time, Son, did you knock over the outhouse?" The little boy thought for a little bit and then answered, "Daddy, I cannot tell a lie. I knocked over the outhouse."

At this point the father turned his son over his knee and proceeded to give him a spanking. The boy cried, "But Daddy, George Washington didn't get a whippin' when he told the truth!"

His dad said, "You're right, Son. But his father wasn't in the cherry tree."

* * *

This particular young man was very shy and after his girlfriend threw her arms around him and kissed him because he bought her a bouquet of flowers, he got up and started to leave! "I'm sorry if I offended you," she said. "Oh no, I'm not offended," he blushed. "I'm just going out to buy more flowers!"

* * *

A little boy had gotten into the habit of saying "darn" of which his mother naturally did not approve. "Dear," she said to the boy, "here's a dime. You can keep it if you promise not to say 'darn' again." He said, "All right, Mom. I promise," and he took the money.

As he lovingly rolled the coin through his fingers, a hopeful look suddenly came into his eyes and he said, "Hey, Mom! I know another word that's worth a dollar!"

* * *

An English teacher wrote on the blackboard, "I ain't had no fun all week." Then she turned to the class and asked how that sentence could be corrected. A little boy in the back of the classroom stood up and said, "Maybe you oughta get a boyfriend!"

* * *

This little boy's mother was having a ladies group meeting and was making tapioca pudding when the phone rang. She left the kitchen to answer it, and her little boy came in to get some BB's for his gun. He reached up in the cabinet for them, the lid came off, and some BB's fell into the tapioca. He heard his mother coming back, so he quickly stirred the BB's into the pudding and ran back outside.

The next morning one of the ladies called to find out how

she made the pudding. She said, "You should know. I got the recipe from you. Why do you ask?" The woman said, "Well, I bent over to pet the cat this morning and shot the canary!"

* * *

One Saturday morning a small boy entered the local bank and with an important air walked up to the cashier's cage and asked to have two cents withdrawn from his savings account. The cashier smiled and complied with the boy's request. Early Monday morning, the same small boy appeared in the bank and put the two cents back into his account. "So, you didn't spend your two cents?" observed the cashier. "Oh no," replied the boy. "A fellow just likes to have a little cash on hand over the weekend."

* * *

A little boy got home from his first day at school. His dad asked him if he learned anything that day. The little boy replied, "Well, I guess I didn't learn enough. I have to go back again tomorrow."

* * *

Two little boys got off the school bus and started walking home. Soon after, a little stone throwing incident started and the second boy was spotted when he threw the rocks back. As he walked into his grandmother's house, she very angrily started pointing her finger at him and scolding him. She said, "Young man, you should have never thrown those rocks back at that boy. You should have come and got me!" He replied, "Why Grandma? You couldn't hit the broad side of a barn!"

* * *

Two babies in the hospital nursery were getting acquainted. "I'm a girl," said one. "I'm a boy," said the other. "How do you know you're a boy?" asked the girl baby. "Wait 'til the nurse leaves the room and I'll show you," he said. When the nurse left, the boy baby pulled up his gown and said, "See, blue booties!"

* * *

A little boy went home from school one day and his mother asked, "How was school today?" The little boy said, "It was awful. Just awful." His mother asked, "Well, what happened that was so bad?" The little boy said, "Well, there was a little mouse running all over and around the classroom. It ran here and there until finally it ran up the teacher's dress! And you know what? I bet the teacher squeezed a quart of water out of that tiny little mouse!"

* * *

There was a small boy who lived out in the country. One evening they had a visitor who the boy had to share his room with. As they got ready for bed, the small boy kneeled down on his side of the bed. Seeing this, the visitor also kneeled down on his side of the bed not wanting the boy to think he didn't say prayers, too. The small boy looked over at him curiously and said, "What are you doing over there?" The visitor replied, "The same thing that you're doing." The boy answered, "My ma is gonna be mad at you. There's no pot on that side."

* * *

One day, instead of serving the usual hot meal, the school cafeteria handed out peanut butter and jelly sandwiches. After lunch, a first grader said to the cafeteria manager, "Thanks, lady. You finally gave us a home-cooked meal!"

* * *

Little Billy's mother took him shopping with her so he could meet Santa Claus. Santa asked Billy what he wanted for Christmas. Very reluctantly, Billy told him he wanted a sled and some skates. "Now write it down so you don't forget!" Billy said.

Several days later, Billy's grandmother took him shopping with her. Quite surprised, Billy met Santa again who called him over and asked him his name. Billy didn't like that much but told him, "Billy." Then Santa said, "And what do you want Santa to bring you for Christmas?" Billy looked at him with disgust and said, "You silly old fool. I told you to write it down!"

※ ※ ※

A little girl was having a hard time in a bookstore selecting which book to give to her mother as a birthday present. The clerk asked, "Well, does she like fiction?" The girl shook her head and said, "I don't think so." The clerk then asked, "How about biography, history, books about art, or humor?" The little girl said, "I'm not sure." Finally, the exasperated clerk demanded, "Well, what on earth *does* she like?" The little girl replied, "Men!"

※ ※ ※

Minnie Pearl is seen here with several performers who played the role of Minnie Pearl for theme park guests in Nashville.

Courtesy of David Skepner

The third grade teacher asked her class to write a composition on the things for which they were thankful. One little boy summed it up very nicely. He wrote, "I'm thankful for my glasses. They keep the big boys from hitting me, and the little girls from kissing me!"

* * *

A proud father took his four-year-old son to visit his mother and newborn brother at the hospital. His dad said to him, "Well, what do you think of your new brother, Son?" The boy said, "He's so red, wrinkled, and ugly, now I see why Mom kept him under her dress so long!"

* * *

A little boy was staying with his aunt. He came up to her at her bridge club and very boldly said, "Auntie, I have to tinkle!" She stood up and took him aside and said, "Jimmy, please don't say 'tinkle' in front of everyone. Say you have to 'whisper' instead." He agreed and later that day she left the nephew with his uncle. Suddenly Jimmy said, "Uncle, I have to whisper!" So his uncle said, "Okay partner, whisper in my ear."

* * *

A small boy brought his teacher a present in a brown paper bag and said, "Guess what it is." She said, "Is it apples?" He said, "No, guess again." She said, "Is it candy?" He said, "No, guess again." She knew the boy's father owned a liquor store and the bottom of the bag was wet, so she asked, "Is it wine?" He laughed and said, "No, it's a puppy!"

* * *

"Why are you crying?" Grandpa asked his grandson. "Daddy won't play cowboys and Indians with me," the boy said. "Well don't cry. I'll play with you," said his grandpa. The boy said, "That's no good, Grandpa. You've already been scalped!"

* * *

A man and his young daughter were in an elevator with several people, including a gorgeous blonde. Just as the elevator door opened, the blonde slapped the man in the face and left in a huff. "I don't like her either," the little girl said to her stunned father. "When she stepped on my foot, I pinched her!"

* * *

On a summer evening during a violent thunderstorm, a mother was tucking her little boy into bed. She was about to turn out the light when he asked in a shaky voice, "Mommy, will you sleep with me tonight?" His mom smiled, gave him a hug and said, "I can't do that, dear. I have to sleep with Daddy."
After a long silence, the little boy said, "The big sissy!"

* * *

A little boy was caught by his teacher as he said a most unsuitable word. "Jeffrey!" she said, "You shouldn't use that word! Where on earth did you hear it?" He answered, "My daddy said it." The teacher replied, "You don't even know what it means!" Jeffrey answered, "Yes I do! It means that Daddy's car won't start!"

* * *

A little boy from the big city was visiting his aunt in Georgia. One day his little girl cousin, about his own age, invited him to go swimming with her. They walked to a little pond outside of town and both hurriedly took off their clothes and jumped into the pond. After splashing around and swimming for a little while, they crawled out onto the grass and proceeded to dry themselves. The little girl looked at her boy cousin critically for a long moment and then she said, "No one ever told me there was so much difference between a Yankee and a Southerner!"

* * *

After watching his mother change the diaper on his newborn sister, a three-year-old boy voiced his concern that she seemed to be missing some parts. In terms the mother thought he would understand, she explained the difference between boys and girls. Then to make sure he understood, she asked him, "Okay son, now what do you have that your new baby sister doesn't?" Smiling broadly, the boy proudly said, "Teeth!"

* * *

A five-year-old boy went for a weekend trip with his grandparents. On the way home, they stopped at a country restaurant for lunch. The little boy left the table to use the restroom by himself and a moment later he returned with a confused look on his face. He said, "Grandma, am I a hen or a rooster?"

* * *

A little boy went with his grandfather to his Great Aunt Sue's funeral. When they returned home, his grandmother asked if Aunt Sue was in a coffin. He thought for a while and said, "She wasn't coffin, but she was definitely a dead duck."

* * *

A father was shopping in a department store with his small daughter when the little girl pulled on his coat sleeve and said, "Daddy, I have to go." "In a few minutes, Dear," said the dad. "I've got to go now," the little girl insisted in a loud voice. A saleslady standing nearby said, "I'll take her." So the two hurried off hand in hand. When they returned the father asked his daughter, "Did you thank the nice lady for being so kind?" "Why should I thank her?" asked the little girl in a loud voice. "She had to go, too."

* * *

A little boy's mom and dad were expecting a new baby and were trying to tell him the good news but weren't sure how. So his mom said, "Junior," and that's as far as she got. She just

Ralph Emery and his Friday night girlfriend Minnie Pearl, enjoying a good joke.

couldn't figure out how to tell him. So she told her husband, "Dear, you're just going to have to do it. I can't." So his dad said, "Junior, I . . . you . . . we.....I mean . . . Grandpa wants to tell you something."

So Grandpa called Junior aside and said, "Now son, for the last few months a great big ol' bird has been flying all around this house, and pretty soon he's going to land right on top of it." Junior spoke up quickly and said, "Oh my gosh, Grandpa, you can't let him do that. Mama's gonna have a baby and it'll scare her to death!"

※ ※ ※

A little boy wrote a report for school about what he did over the winter break.

He wrote, "We always spend Christmas with Grandma and Grandpa. They used to live here in a big brick house, but grandpa got retarded and they moved to Florida. They live in a place with a lot of other retarded people. They live in a little tin hut. They ride big three-wheel bicycles. They go to a building they call the wrecked room, but it looks like it's fixed now. They play games there and do exercises, but not very well. There is a swimming pool and they go into it and just stand there with their hats on. I guess they don't know how to swim. My grandma used to bake cookies and stuff, but I guess she forgot how. They all go to restaurants that are fast. Nobody cooks anymore. As you go into the park where they live there is a doll house with a man sitting in it. He watches all day so they can't get out without him seeing them. They wear badges with their names on them. I guess they don't know who they are.

My grandma says that grandpa worked hard all of his life and earned his retardment. I wish they would move back home, but I guess the man in the doll house won't let them out."

* * *

On the first day of school the kindergarten teacher told her class, "If anyone has to go to the bathroom, just hold up two fingers." After a quiet moment, one little boy asked, "How's that gonna help?"

* * *

A nursery school teacher was delivering a station wagon load of kids home one day when a fire truck went zooming past. The children noticed that right on the front seat was a Dalmatian dog. Seeing this, the children started arguing over what the dog's duties were. The first said, "They use him to keep the crowds back!" Another said, "No way! He's just for good luck!" A third child firmly replied, "You're all wrong. They use him to find the fire plug!"

* * *

A kindergarten class was sitting on their blankets when the teacher asked, "Students, how can you tell Ronald McDonald from anyone else in a crowd?" An anxious young boy raised his hand and said, "He's the one with sesame seeds on his buns!"

11.
The "Propeller" Set

Maybe they don't move about as quickly as they used to, and maybe they don't hear as well as they once did either. But the senior set of the Switch certainly gets around. Well, some seem to get around more than others, but they've obviously cooled their jets a little.

I don't know whether it's the mountain air or just a healthy way of living, but the elders I've heard about from out in the country near Grinder's Switch certainly are a lively bunch. Well, come to think of it, I'm relatively certain it's not the air because at the wrong time of day downwind from Uncle Nabob's goat farm, the breeze can stop the hands of time. So it must be the way of life.

You see, the pace in Grinder's Switch always seems to be a little slower than it is in the big city—even for Minnie Pearl. From the stories she has told, I don't think folks there get old, they just become more relaxed over time, kind of like the elastic in a cheap girdle. But that's not to say that the folks are lazy. They're simply smart enough now to wait for life to pass them by instead of running after it like a spurred quarter horse. You know, somebody in Grinder's Switch once started some gossip that every man around the place had been kissing Minnie. She said, "Well I wanna tell you right here and now that there ain't a speck of truth to it! I don't have time to go around like that. But I'm sure mighty grateful for the rumor!"

But in a turnaround of country hospitality where beauty comes before age, Minnie's boyfriend Hezzie once overheard a fellow talking about his sweetheart. The man said that Minnie

had the face of a sixteen-year-old girl. Old Hezzie looked over at Minnie on the porch and said to the fellow, "Well she better give it back to her quick 'cause Minnie's gettin' it so beat up, pretty soon the girl won't have it back!"
Uh-oh, I think I hear the old biplane firing up. All aboard!

* * *

Old Sut Simpson, he's a feller at Grinder's Switch. He's finally got around to proposing to Aggie Abernathy, she's a lady spinster up there. Ooo-wee! I tell ya', Grinder's Switch has got more lady spinsters up there than I ever saw! I'm fixin' to move up there myself. When Sut went in to tell Aggie's pappy about it, Sut said, "I'd like to marry Aggie, but she said she don't want to leave her mammy. Aggie's pappy said, "Shucks, son, that ain't no problem. You can just take both of them with you if you want to!"

* * *

When it comes to girls, most men are like adolescents. Adolescent is when a boy stops collectin' stamps and starts playin' post office!
I had this old friend who said he quit playin' post office a long time ago. When I asked him, "Why? Don't you get fun out of bein' called to the post office and for some mail and then kissin' a girl in a dark hall?" He said, "I used to. But the last time I played, all the girls sent me back to the dead letter office!" I told him, "That's what those girls get for playin' post office with a third-class male!"

* * *

My feller Hezzie, he's gone into a new kind of business in Grinder's Switch here recent. He's gone into the antique business for a hobby. I might not have found out about it, but I overheard somebody sayin' that Hezzie was "goin' around with an old relic!"
I thought I'd help Hezzie out, so when I heard that Lucifer Hucklehead had an old, old antique bedstead that he wanted

to sell, I went over to see it. I asked Lucifer if he was sure it was a genuine antique, and he said, "I'll have you know that George Washington and Abraham Lincoln slept in this bed on the same night." I said, "Why Lucifer, it would be impossible for Washington and Lincoln to sleep in this bed on the same night." And he said, "Why is that? Ain't it a double bed?"

* * *

An older lady was out shopping when she noticed a very expensive boutique advertising, "Dresses and hats on sale!" She couldn't resist and went in and started trying on dresses and hats.

After awhile, she found only a hat that she really liked and bought it. When she stepped back outside, a fierce wind had picked up as she walked down the street to the bus stop. While she was standing there, she was quite worried that the wind might blow off her brand new hat. So she held on to it with both hands. Not paying mind to anything else, she soon felt a tap on her shoulder and turned to see a young man there who said, "Excuse me, ma'am, but why are you just holding your hat while your dress is blowing clear up to your elbows?" The woman replied, "Son, I've had what's under this dress for almost eighty-six years, but I've only had this hat for an hour!"

* * *

An upper-class ladies club out in Los Angeles invited a woman author to recite one of her works at its monthly meeting. She proceeded to recite one of her woeful "triple tearjerkers" so well that the entire assembly broke out in tears! That is, all but one lady who sat dry-eyed and stiff as a board throughout the entire recital. Afterwards, the author walked up and asked her why she hadn't cried too. The lady stopped cold and answered, "Oh! I'm not a member."

* * *

A old man's house caught on fire and he was hanging out of a window yelling for help. A neighbor outside hollered back,

"Just dial 9-11 and the fire department will come!" So he ducked back in, grabbed the phone and tried and tried but the fire department got there too late and his house burned down. The same neighbor asked what had happened, and the old man said, "I found the nine but I never could find the eleven!"

* * *

An older lady went on a routine visit to the new young doctor in town. After he checked her over he embarrassingly asked, "Because of your age I have to know if you have S.E.X." She said, "Wait just a minute and I'll see." So she opened the door to the waiting room and yelled out to her husband, "Honey, the doctor wants to know if we have S.E.X." He replied, "No! All we have is Blue Cross and Blue Shield."

* * *

An elderly lady had spent some time in the hospital but was finally sent home. Soon after that she was visited by her minister and while he was there, he saw a little dish of peanuts on the table in the living room. As they sat there talking, he kept eating the nuts until they were all gone. As he started to leave he turned and said to the old lady, "I'm sorry I ate all of your peanuts." "Oh that's all right," she replied. "I couldn't eat them anyway. You see, my teeth are bad, and it took me all the morning just to suck the chocolate off of them!"

* * *

An elderly man was on his deathbed, and his wife was sitting beside him lovingly holding his hand. The old man looked at her and said softly, "Honey, do you remember the time our house was washed away by the floodwaters and we lost all of our belongings? You were there by my side, weren't you?" His wife said, "Yes dear, I remember." The old man looked at her again and said, "And remember the time our barn burned down and we lost all of our animals and all of the hay? You were there by my side then, too, right?" His wife nodded lovingly and said, "Yes dear, I remember." With that the old man raised up in his bed and said, "Honey, now you're with me by my side as I lay on my deathbed, holding my hand, and I can't help but wonder, could it be that you're jinxed?"

* * *

An old gentleman went to an auction and bought himself a big grandfather clock. He was feeling pretty good, so he decided to carry it home. As he walked down the street, a drunk walked by and bumped into the man making him drop the clock. The old man said, "Why don't you watch where you're walking? Look at what you've done!" And the drunk said, "Well, why can't you just wear a wristwatch like everybody else?"

* * *

A police officer pulled an elderly woman motorist to the side of the road and exclaimed, "When I saw you come zooming around that curve I said to myself that you had to be pushing sixty-five!" "Well, you're wrong, officer!" protested the elderly woman driver. "This hat just makes me look older!"

* * *

There was this old man who suddenly couldn't hear at all out of one ear. He decided he'd better go see his doctor. When he got into the doctor's office he said, "Doc, all of a sudden I can't hear at all in my left ear!" So the doctor said, "Get up on the table and I'll take a look." Instantly the doctor said, "I think I know what your trouble is already." The old man said, "You do?" The doctor nodded, pulled a suppository out of his ear, and said, "Here's the problem." The old man looked up at the doctor and said, "Oh my Lord! *Now* I know where my hearing aid is!"

* * *

Sam and Bill were best friends and since they were both in their eighties, they made a bargain that whoever died first would try to come back and tell the other what the afterlife was like. Shortly after making the deal, Sam passed away. A few nights later as Bill was lying in his bed, he heard a familiar voice coming in through his window. "Bill! Bill!" The old man sat up and said, "My God, Sam, is that you?" "Yes, and I've got to tell you that the afterlife is marvelous! Simply marvelous!" "Well, tell me about it," Bill urged.

"In the morning we eat breakfast and then spend hours making love. Then we eat lunch and spend many more hours making love. Finally, we eat dinner and make love again!" "Holy cow!" said Bill. "I can't wait to die and go to Heaven!" "Heaven?" retorted Sam. "Heck, I'm outside. I died and came back as a rabbit!"

An elderly man was sitting on a park bench crying as hard he could when a policeman stopped and asked what was wrong. The man replied, "It's my birthday and I'm ninety years old today." The policeman said, "Well, I sure hope I'm in as good a shape as you when I'm ninety." "Well," the elderly man continued, "do you know I'm married to a twenty-four-year-old girl?" "Wow!" the policeman said. "I definitely hope I'm in the same position as you when I'm ninety! But everything sounds so good for you. Why are you still crying?" The elderly man replied, "Well, they say the mind is the first thing to go and now I can't find my way home!"

* * *

A self-educated old farmer who had never owned a fancy car was looking at a brand new Cadillac. The salesman said, "This particular model will cost you $30,000." So the farmer reached into his pocket and counted out $30,000. When the salesman saw this he said, "Well, if you're paying cash, I can give you a discount." Not knowing what he meant, the farmer asked for a minute and went next door to a beauty shop. Inside, he asked the beautiful girl who worked there, "Do you know what the word *discount* means?" She explained, "It means to take something off." So he asked her, "Well, how much would you take off if I gave you $30,000?" She answered, "Would you mind if I kept my earrings on?"

* * *

A man and his wife were on vacation in the husband's home-town. They hadn't been back there for forty years. They enjoyed the trip so much that they went back the next year. They went to the same parks, cafes, and motel where they visited the year before. The wife even went back to the same beauty shop. While she was there, the owner asked the lady if she was from their town. She said, "I don't know you, but you look familiar. Have you ever been here before?"

The woman replied, "Yes I have, but it's been a year ago this month since you've done my hair." Another lady in the shop in a sweet, small, elderly voice piped up and said, "Well I'll be, Honey! It sure did keep good!"

* * *

An elderly man and wife were watching television when he got up to go to the kitchen during a commercial. He said, "I'm going to get some ice cream." His wife said, "Well, while you're in there, would you bring me a dish of vanilla ice cream?" He said, "Okay," to which she replied, "You'd better write that down so you don't forget." He said, "That's such an easy thing to remember, I won't forget." She said, "Do you mind putting some chocolate syrup on it?" Again, he said he would and again she said back, "Don't you think you should write that down so you don't forget?" A little annoyed, he said, "I won't forget." Then she said, "While you're at it, please put some whipped cream, nuts, and a cherry on the top." Again she said to write it down so he wouldn't forget, and he said, "I won't forget! You want vanilla ice cream with chocolate syrup, whipping cream, nuts, and a cherry on it." Surprised that he remembered, she said, "That's right!"

About a half hour later he came back and handed her two fried eggs. She looked up at him and said, "Where have you been? And where's my toast?"

* * *

There's this eighty-year-old man in the neighborhood who is quite active for his age and has a sense of humor that never seems to stop. One day while he was out mowing his lawn, a car pulled up in the driveway and a pretty young lady motioned for him to come over to the car. He walked over and the young beauty said, "Mister, I just moved into the neighborhood and don't know anyone in town. What would you charge to come over and cut my grass?"

He thought for a moment and said, "Well, I don't know, miss, but the lady here lets me sleep with her!"

* * *

Two old-timers from the backwoods were discussing their first football game. The first asked, "How'd you like the game?" His friend said, "Well, it was pretty good but it seemed like an awful lot of trouble over twenty-five cents." The other said, "What do you mean?" to which he replied, "All through the game everybody kept yelling, 'Get the quarterback!'"

* * *

There were seven old ladies who walked into a bar, sat down at a table, and ordered seven shots of whiskey and one small glass of water. No sooner had the waitress delivered the order, than the ladies again ordered seven shots of whiskey and one small glass of water. This continued for a little while until the bartender couldn't stand it anymore.

He walked over to the old ladies and said, "I'm sorry to bother you ladies, but I'm curious as to why you can keep ordering seven shots of whiskey and only one little glass of water." One of the ladies turned to him and said, "Son, when you get to be our age it's a lot easier to hold your liquor than it is to hold your water!"

* * *

Courtesy of Jim Hagans

You were watching country royalty when the Queen of Country Comedy and the King of the Grand Ole Opry, Roy Acuff, took the stage together.

There was an old couple sitting on the front porch in their rocking chairs. The old fellow looked over and said, "Maw, what's happened to our sex relations?" She said, "I don't know, Paw. We haven't heard from 'em since last Christmas."

* * *

There were two old men sitting on the front porch of their nursing home, rocking in their chairs and watching people pass by. Then one of the men said, "You know, I think I've got to get up. My hind end is falling asleep!" The other said, "I believe you. I think I just heard it snoring!"

* * *

Two elderly ladies, who hadn't seen each other in years, were visiting over a cup of coffee. One said to the other, "You know, as long and as well as I have known you, I can't for the life of me remember your name. Please tell me what it is!"

The other lady thought quietly for a moment and then asked, "How soon do you have to know?"

* * *

An elderly couple got married and decided to go back to the bride's house. After dinner and a glass of wine, they went into the bedroom for the night. As the wife went to the bathroom, she stopped at the bureau and took a pill. Her husband said, "Mary, what are you taking that pill for?" She smiled and replied, "It makes me feel young!" She went into the bathroom and John jumped up, went to the bureau, and took all the pills left in the bottle. Afterwards, they both fell fast asleep.

In the morning, Mary woke up and found that John was not in bed. She looked everywhere and finally saw him sitting outside on the curb. She said, "John, what are you doing out here?" He looked at her with tears in his eyes and said, "I missed the school bus!"

* * *

A widow who lived alone was asked by a friend if she ever got lonesome. She replied, "Heavens no! I've got four men in my life!" The friend asked her, "Who on earth are they?" She replied, "Well, I get up with Charlie Horse, I have lunch with Arthur Itis, I spend afternoons with Will Power, and I go to bed with Ben Gay."

* * *

An old spinster's cat cornered a mouse in her kitchen. Just as the cat was about to kill its prey, the mouse said to the woman, "If you call your cat off, I'll grant you three wishes!" The woman agreed and started wishing.

"First, I wish for a million dollars," said the spinster. "Granted," said the mouse, and he handed her the money. "Now," said the woman, "I want to be young and beautiful," and instantly she was transformed into a young beauty. "And finally," she said, "turn my cat into a tall, handsome prince lying next to me in bed." With a poof her wish was granted.

"I'm so happy," said the spinster to her prince. "I'm glad," said the prince. "But now aren't you sorry you had me fixed?"

✳ ✳ ✳

Three elderly women were discussing their lives and getting older. One of them said, "I have this problem. Sometimes when I go to the refrigerator, I can't remember whether I'm taking something out or putting it in." "That's nothing," said another. "I find myself standing at the stairs wondering if I'm going up or if I've just come down."

The third woman said, "Well, I'm thankful I don't have any such problems," and she knocked on wood and said, "Would you both excuse me. There's someone at the door."

✳ ✳ ✳

An older couple that was getting on in years were experiencing some troubles in the bedroom. So they decided to ask Dr. Ruth for help. She asked the man how often he got frisky and he replied, "Oh, almost every night!" Dr. Ruth said, "Really?" The man's wife quickly replied, "That's right. Almost on Monday and almost on Tuesday, almost on Wednesday..."

✳ ✳ ✳

A young woman boarded a bus carrying a baby. As she was paying her fare, the bus driver said to her, "Lady, that is the ugliest baby I've ever seen!" She burst into tears and took a seat in the back of the bus. Seated next to her was an elderly man with glasses. He said, "I don't know what that driver said to you, but you oughta go tell him off, and I'll hold your monkey while you do it!"

✳ ✳ ✳

A forgetful little old lady was talking to a young friend of hers who asked how she was getting on. The lady replied, "It's really not so bad being senile. Now I get to hide my own Easter eggs!"

* * *

A crowd stood around the 100-foot diving tower at the fairgrounds waiting for the featured performer. Finally, a feeble old man walked out leaning on a cane.

"Good evening," he said. "I'm ninety-nine years old and I'm going to amaze you! I'm going to climb to the top of that 100-foot tower and dive into a teeny-tiny tub of water! Are you ready?"

The audience members begged, "Don't do it!" The little old man said, "Okay! Next show at ten o'clock."

* * *

Three old men were discussing the ideal way of dying. The first man who was eighty years old said, "I'd like to crash in a car going 80 mph!" The second man who was eighty-five said, "I'd like to crash in a plane going 400 mph!" The third man who was ninety-five years old said, "I'd like to be shot by a jealous husband."

* * *

Two old ladies went to the liquor store and bought a bottle of whiskey. After having several nips, the two decided to go to a local baseball game. When they arrived they were being quite loud disturbing a man in the grandstands. After several innings another latecomer arrived and sat in the same section. He noticed how loud the pair of women were and asked the first man, "Can you tell me what inning it is?" Looking towards the two women the gentleman replied, "Well, I'm pretty sure we're at the bottom of the fifth and the bags are loaded!"

12.
Little Jimmy Dickens Remembers Minnie

Little Jimmy Dickens may be small in stature, but he can certainly get some of the biggest laughs on the Opry stage whether he's telling a catchy joke or singing one of his signature comedic songs. Jimmy told me that when he first came to the Opry, he and Minnie became almost immediate friends. "She took me under her wing," he said. "She would watch me perform onstage, and I would use some little gags, and when I got done she would ask me if I wanted to get a better laugh out of a joke." As he put it, he had the intelligence to listen to her when she would show him how to tell the joke her way. "And it worked every time!" he admitted.

Like so many of Minnie's friends, Little Jimmy said he could go on forever about her. But being the country gentleman that he is, and knowing that books are limited to a finite number of pages, he spared us and just told his favorite Grinder's Switch story. It is, not surprisingly, about Brother.

> You see, Brother wasn't wrapped too tight. One day he was goin' down the road draggin' a big, heavy log chain over his shoulder. After awhile, someone stopped and asked him, "Why on earth are you draggin' that log chain down the road?" And Brother said, "Well, have you ever tried to push one?"

13.
"Little Johnny" Goes Country

I'm sure that Little Jimmy certainly is no kin to Little Johnny. But the troublesome youngun always seems to be in the limelight, too. Minnie didn't make a habit of telling Little Johnny jokes, but every once in awhile when she visited us at the television show, one or two of the famed fables of the notorious youth would become the topic of conversation.

Little Johnny is somewhat of a comedic chameleon. He's been a boy from the city or the country, and for all I know he's international. It seems entirely possible that on the side roads of the German autobahn they're telling Little Johann sagas or that Little Giovanni is all the rage in the Italian countryside.

Nevertheless, Johnny has managed to sneak his way into the wisecracks of Grinder's Switch, at least in this collection. Though he may never have actually set foot in one of the bear traps surrounding the town, these are a few of the tales we snared.

* * *

Little Johnny asked his grandmother how old she was. She said, "You should never ask a lady that." Then he asked her how much she weighed. Again she said, "You should never ask a lady that." Then Johnny asked her why she and Grandpa slept in separate rooms and she said, "I can't tell you that either."

So Little Johnny being a bright young man, got an idea. He ran upstairs and looked at his grandma's driver's license. Then he went to his grandma and said, "Grandma, I know how old you are." She said, "You do?" He said, "Yep. You're seventy-five. I also know how much you weigh." She asked, "How much?" And he said, "A hundred thirty-five! And I also know why Grandpa don't sleep with you no more. You got an 'F' in sex!"

* * *

Little Johnny received a very bad report card. When he got home from school, he waited anxiously for his dad, a lawyer, to come home from work. When his dad got there, Little Johnny handed his report card to his father and said, "Dad, I want you to look over this report card very carefully to see if we can sue for defamation of character!"

* * *

The teacher thought Little Johnny had a bad habit of stretching the truth and decided to try to break him of it. She said, "Johnny, as I looked out my back window this morning I saw a big grizzly bear in my trash can! And about that time, a little black dog came around the corner, grabbed that bear by the leg, and pulled him out of the trash can. They fought, and do you know that little black dog killed that bear right there? Now Johnny, do you believe that story?"

"I sure do," said Johnny. "That's *my* little black dog and that's the fourth bear he's killed this week!"

* * *

The school bell rang just as Little Johnny started eating a popsicle and since he didn't want to waste it, he stuck it in his pants pocket. Back in the classroom, the teacher asked little Vicky, "What do they call someone who lives at the North Pole?" She said, "An Eskimo." Then the teacher asked little Teresa, "What do they call someone who lives in Mexico?" She said, "A Mexican." Then the teacher asked Little Johnny what they called someone who lives in Europe. Johnny said,

"I don't know." Then smart little Mary behind Johnny said, "European." And Johnny said, "I am not! That's a popsicle meltin' in my pocket!"

* * *

Little Johnny asked his mother if he could get a dog. His mom said, "How about a little baby brother instead?" Johnny replied, "Oh goody!" So Johnny went to school the next day all excited telling the kids and his teacher about his little brother.

When Johnny went home his mom asked, "Do you want to feel your little brother?" Curious, he did what she said and placed his hands on her stomach and sure enough, Johnny could feel some little arms and legs there.

So the next day, Johnny went to school all down in the dumps. His teacher asked, "What's the matter Johnny? Aren't you still excited about your little brother?" Johnny said, "We're not going to have no little brother." His teacher said, "Why not?" Johnny said, "'Cause Mommy ate it!"

* * *

The teacher asked three children in school, two boys and one girl, what they wanted to do when they grew up. The first little boy, Billy, said, "When I grow up to be a man, I'm going to Japan. If I think I can, I know I can." Next, Sally said, "Teacher, when I grow up to be a lady, I'm not going to Japan. I'm gonna stay home and have a baby. If I think I can, I know I can."

Then Johnny jumped up and said, "Teacher, when I grow up to be a man, I'm not going to Japan. I'm staying home to help Sally with her plan. If I think I can, I know I can."

* * *

Little Johnny told his father that he and Suzy were going to get married. Johnny was six years old and Suzy was five. His dad said, "Well son, if you and Suzy are getting married, we need to have a man-to-man talk. Where are you all going to

A country girl at heart, Dinah Shore (center), joins Cousin Minnie Pearl and Opry legend Roy Acuff on stage.

live?" Johnny said, "Oh, we're gonna live with you and Mama." His dad said, "Fine. You have a place to live. What about finances?" Johnny said, "Suzy gets fifty cents a week and I get seventy-five. We've got plenty of money." "Good," said his dad. "Then finances are settled. But son, you know married people have children."

Little Johnny said, "Oh yes, Suzy and I talked about that too. If she lays any eggs, I'm gonna step on them!"

✳ ✳ ✳

Little Johnny was on his way to school one day but decided to take a shortcut across a farmer's field instead of using the road. On his way he tore his pants getting through a barbed wire fence. After mending his britches the best that he could, he proceeded on to school.

As he was arriving late, the teacher said, "Johnny, I see you're a little behind this morning!" To which Johnny replied, "Yeah, but you wouldn't if I had another safety pin!"

14.
Jimmy C. Newman
Remembers Minnie

We talked backstage one night where Jimmy C. Newman reminisced that Minnie seemed to be intrigued with the Cajun culture, as were many entertainers at that time. He remembered that Sarah Cannon and her husband, Henry, loved Cajun food and rice. They had been to Louisiana and enjoyed the cuisine firsthand. Jimmy says he first met Minnie Pearl in 1956 after he came to the Grand Ole Opry. As he put it, "She was a seasoned entertainer, and I was very green, having only worked the honky-tonks of Louisiana." He said that he could have educated her on that arena, but it would have been entirely unnecessary. "I had a lot of respect for her and she was very nice to me. I think she was nice to everybody," Jimmy said. "When Minnie would take the stage, the reception was unbelievable."

Thinking back some more, he told me the story of how Minnie had gotten a new poodle, and she wanted to give it a French name. So she asked him to help her choose one. Jimmy had a Cajun friend in Louisiana with the last name of LaFleur, so he jokingly suggested that she name the dog "LaFleur." After a good laugh, he confessed, "And that's what she named it, LaFleur!"

The last time he heard Minnie Pearl tell his favorite joke was with Ralph Emery.

Back in Grinder's Switch, Brother and another guy went into business selling hay. They'd buy it for one price, haul it on the truck, and then sell it for less than they bought it. One day they got together to talk things over and Brother told his partner, "We gotta do something about this hay deal. We're just not makin' any money! We're buyin' it for one price and we're sellin' it for a lot lower price!" His partner looked at him and said, "Well, I guess we better get a bigger truck!"

There are some variations on a second joke he remembered, but this one is as close to a reasonable version that we could agree upon.

One day the passengers on a train were greeted by a masked train robber. He told everyone, "Reach for the sky and keep your hands held high!" He proceeded to walk through the car frisking each passenger and emptying their bags and pockets of money. He arrived at this old gal and began to frisk her. When he found she had no money or jewelry, he started to move on to the next person. She quickly said, "Excuse me Mr. Robber! I know I don't have any money, but if you frisk me again I'll write you a check!"

15.
Just Don't Ask Us For Directions

There are definitely some things you would ask a country woman or gentleman for advice on. How do you get that pie crust to be so flaky? Do you think the fish are biting on crank baits or live minnows today? Is it gonna rain? But when you come to the crossroads of your rural excursion, don't ever ask for directions.

Country folks have a special flair for getting to and fro. The only problem is, if you haven't kept up with the geographical landscape changes for oh, say the last fifty years, you're liable to end up right back where you started from: an old front porch with two men rocking in cane chairs or playing a heated game of checkers. "Do you know how to get to the Hucklehead farm?"

"Well, first you take the old church road down to where the creek rose up and flooded Poker Face Perkins's storm cellar on the bend and washed it clean away. Then go about a half a mile or two until you come to where the old oak tree was that got struck by lightning and ended up in the Twitchem's backyard. That is, before they moved and cut the tree down for kindlin'. Right then you're almost part way to the spot where Moonshine McGinny's first still was, until revenuers chopped it up and he moved it over to the valley, which is about a mile or three from the road that *used* to lead to the Hucklehead farm, that is, until it got washed out by the second flood. In that case, don't go the way I just told ya."

Get the idea?

The other thing country folks, like the residents of Grinder's Switch, have in common is a certain curiosity about the "big" city. The "big" city doesn't have to be someplace like New York or Chicago. It can be anyplace that has more than one main street with more than one working traffic signal. It's also a place where the girls are a little more friendly and the men are, well, a lot like an apple right off the tree . . . fresh and already picked over.

Grinder's Switch is also well known for its social gatherings. Now a social gathering might consist of anything from a dance, a ball game, singing, a traveling circus, town meetings, or a county fair. They're called gatherings because people assemble from all over to be a part of the commotion. It's social because folks hobnob and mingle which gives the local gossip mill kernels to grind for weeks on end!

The thing to remember is that country folks are simple people with a history of doing things a certain way. They know the difference between solid common sense and just good horse sense (horse sense by its nonodoriferous definition, of course). So if you think you can easily pull the wool over the eyes of one of the Switch's denizens, you'd better be ready for a good fleecing yourself! Because if there's more than one way to skin a polecat, they probably know it best.

We all went to a carnival and a sideshow playing way over in Shady Grove this past week. Hezzie drove us over in his car and it seemed like we'd been drivin' an awful long time. So I said to Hezzie, "How are we doin'? Are we lost?" And Hezzie said, "Yeah, we're lost. But we sure are makin' good time, ain't we?"

Well, that Hezzie, he's a smart boy. Ain't no flies on Hezzie. Not since we got DDT. Well sir, we finally we got to the carnival, and who should Uncle Nabob run into there at the carnival but an ol' flame of his. Well, she's a fire-eater there at the carnival. It didn't take Aunt Ambrosia long to get them separated though.

She knew if Uncle Nabob stayed around long enough with that fire-eater, they was bound to cook up somethin'!

But there was a fella there at that carnival and he offered anybody twenty-five dollars if they could stay in the boxin' ring with him for three rounds. So we sent Brother in there, and after the first round, Uncle Nabob ran up to brother, who was all beat up, and said, "Keep going Brother! That there fella, he ain't laid a glove on you!" And Brother said, "Then you better keep a eye on that referee 'cause somebody's just been whoopin' the daylights outta me!" I was kinda surprised Brother didn't do no better than he did. Everybody at Grinder's Switch knows that Brother is an expert at the rabbit punch. Maybe it only works when Brother's fighting rabbits.

My boyfriend Hezzie didn't stay for the boxing match. He said he wanted to go and see the moving picture show. He was watching a moving picture show, alright. He was watching a tattooed lady doing a hoochie-coochie show!

* * *

At the town meeting last week, there were several suggestions made. Some of 'em said buy Brother a one-way ticket to Mexico. Then somebody made a motion to make Main Street in Grinder's Switch a one-way street. But it was voted down after it was pointed out that if anybody drove outta town there wouldn't be no way to get back!

* * *

We had a social the other evenin' in Grinder's Switch. I got a brand new dress for the occasion. The lady that sold it to me said it was an "indoors dress." When I looked at it, I said there seems to be more *outdoors* than there is indoors! I wouldn't wear it!

Hezzie and me danced together at the social. I must say that Hezzie ain't a very good dancer. But oo-oo! Can he intermission! It was right after that, Hezzie and some old boy up there in Grinder's Switch had a big fight about who was gonna take me home. They tossed a coin and Hezzie lost. So Hezzie had to take me home.

The Henry Twitcherts was at the dance. They were just married. Oh, it's so sweet. It was the first marriage for both of them. He's seventy-five and she's eighty years old. Instead of rice, they threw vitamin pills at 'em!

Uncle Nabob and Aunt Ambrosia was there at the social too. They had another one of their arguments. Lately he's been beatin' her. And she didn't mind it for herself, it's the children. They beat her too! But you know, Uncle Nabob and Aunt Ambrosia, I never will forget that time they got a brand new clock, and the first night they had it, right after the clock struck twelve, it struck thirteen. And Uncle Nabob said, "Get up, Brosie, and light the lamp! It's later than I ever knowed it to be!"

* * *

This week we decided we'd better take Brother up to Nashville and try to get him a job. So I took him to one of the places and the man said he'd give Brother a job. He said, "I can start you at thirty dollars a week, and in five years you'll get two hundred!" Brother said, "That's fine. I'll be back in five years!"

* * *

There's been a terrible wind just a blowin' all week up at the Switch. And today was the windiest day yet. You sure can tell the country girls from the city girls on a windy day. The country girls hold on to their skirts—the city girls hold on to their hats!

* * *

Brother is always tryin' to invent something. Most recently he invented a liquid that will dissolve anything! That liquid will dissolve anything on earth. There's just one trouble. He can't find nothin' to keep it in!

* * *

The circus came to Grinder's Switch. And they had that there Mademoiselle Fifi, the one that don't speak nothin' but

French. But her motions can be understood in any language! She was the one that Brother was talkin' to. Someone asked me did Brother actually speak French. I said, "Well, not much. Just enough to get his face slapped."

Lath Plodgett up there in Grinder's Switch has a son who joined the circus. They shoot him out of a cannon. Folks say he does pretty well for money, too. He gets eighty cents a mile.

You know, Uncle Nabob used to work in the circus. He used to slide down a wire hanging by his teeth. Until one night, his teeth made it but he didn't!

*** * ***

The Grinder's Switch Sluggers opened the baseball season with the strongest team in the league: The Piney Point Polecats. What do you know. They skunked us again!

We got a lot of good players, though, in the old Smokey league and sometimes there's a baseball scout from one of them big league teams there to watch 'em. One time Grandpappy Buskem come hustlin' down in his Confederate uniform when he heard there was a Yankee scout there.

Our ballpark at Grinder's Switch is the funniest thing. See, it's in Flood Sneed's pasture and there's always a few cows roamin' around in the outfield. So, we have a ground rule that says you can only go as far as third base if the ball hits the cow. Uncle Nabob says its the only park in the league where you can get a triple for hittin' a one bagger!

An old feller was tellin' us about a player on his home team. He said they got a player who runs like Mickey Mantle, throws like Bob Lemon, and hits like Stan Musial. I said, "He must be quite a feller! He said, "Feller nothin'! It's my gal Suzy. She's a pitcher. She's got a good fastball, but her curves ain't so hot!"

Our biggest problem in Grinder's Switch is to get one of them fellers that stands back there with a birdcage in front of his face and a mat down the front. The call 'em umpires. You see, in Grinder's Switch when they start yellin', "Kill the umpire!" somebody starts diggin' a grave.

We finally got that big feller, Mad Mountain Murdock, to be the umpire. He's a great big feller. A blacksmith. But it was a mistake. He made a decision that the Polecats didn't like and they started gangin' up on old Mad Mountain. So he give 'em a tongue lashin' and that broke up that game. My friend said, "You mean those pantywaists quit just because old Mad Mountain gave 'em a bawlin' out?" I told him, "You don't understand. When Mad Mountain gives a tongue lashin' he does it with a wagon tongue!"

* * *

Lucifer Hucklehead almost got his block knocked off for tryin' to give his wife a compliment. One of those government farm bureau fellers come by and told Lucifer how fortunate he was to have such a hard working wife. And Lucifer said, "I sure am. I wish I had two more just like her!"

While this government feller was callin' on Lucifer, he got real poetical like. And he was a pointin' out at the field and he said, "Ah, the wonders of nature. The good earth is turned warm by the sun and moistened by the summer rains, and the seed springs forth from the soil and soon there appears a field of waving corn. It's a miracle!" And Lucifer said, "It sure is! I planted rhubarb!"

* * *

There was this old farmer up in Grinder's Switch that just didn't have any sense. Why, he couldn't pull a fast one in a milkin' contest! In fact, he's been doin' so much milkin' lately that when he shakes hands he does it one finger at a time!

* * *

Well, now Lucifer Hucklehead, he's a real good friend of ours at Grinder's Switch, he's a real nice fella. He's been up to his what ya call "experiments" again. He tried to cross a parrot with a hen so that instead of cacklin', the chickens would just yell, "Come on over here Lucifer! I just laid an egg!" That was like that time he crossed a owl with a goat and got a "hootn' nanny!"

Well, Lucifer though, he's a smart feller, but one time he planted the potatoes too close to the onions in his garden. Them poor old potatoes just cried their eyes out, needless to say.

Backstage at the Grand Ole Opry House television host Keith Bilbrey and "Cousin" Minnie Pearl share a laugh.

Me and Uncle Nabob went up to New York, and while we was up there everybody was awful nice to us and tried to entertain us and everything. Some of the fellers asked Uncle Nabob if he wanted to play a game that Uncle Nabob never had heard tell of. They called it golf. Uncle Nabob asked how to play it. So one of the fellers said, "Well, you take a little stick and knock a little white ball around acres of grass!" Uncle Nabob said, "That game ain't for me. I ain't gonna start chasin' no little white ball around until I'm too old to chase anything else!"

They sure do go fast up there in New York City. I'm tellin' you right now. It's a caution the way folks up there hurry and scurry and helter and skelter. I declare if anybody in New York ever got the seven-year itch he'd scratch it out in a year and a half!

But they don't waste no time comin' to the point in the big city. There was a sign in one of their store windows that sold corsets. That sign said, "If you're built like a house, let us build you a foundation!"

* * *

Well, the news in Grinder's Switch is that Brother's gone off to college. Somebody asked me what he was studying. I told 'em, "He ain't studyin' anything. They're studyin' him!"

* * *

A carpenter and his contractor drove their truck into the local lumberyard one day to get a load of wood. The carpenter got out, went to the counter, and first asked for some two-by-fours, eight feet long. The salesman asked, "How many?" "Just a minute," the carpenter said, and went back to the truck and asked the contractor. He came back and said, "A hundred eighty!" "OK," said the salesman. "I also want some one-by-eights, ten feet long," said the man. Again, the salesman asked how many. "Just a minute," and the man again went to the truck and asked the contractor, came back and said, "Two hundred forty!" "Is there anything else?" asked the salesman. Thinking he was getting smart now, and having asked the contractor already, the man said, "I need four hundred one-by-sixes!" This time the salesman asked, "How long do you need 'em?" The man scratched his head, went back to the truck and returned to the salesman and proudly said, "We need 'em a long time. We're building a house!"

* * *

A man who lived in the loony bin was standing in the institution yard near the road when a farmer drove by with a horse and wagon. The patient called out to the farmer, who stopped. He asked, "What do you have in the wagon?" The farmer said, "I've got a load of manure." The patient asked, "So what are you going to do with it?" The farmer replied, "I'm gonna put it on my strawberries!" The patient shook his head and said back, "I put cream and sugar on mine and they think *I'm* crazy!"

* * *

Old man Smith always said, "When I die, I want to be buried at the top of the hill at the edge of town!" Well, one day he developed a terrible cough and cold and died. So, as he requested, they took his coffin way up to the top of the hill at the edge of town, but as they set it down, the coffin started to slide down the hill! It slid all the way down the hill picking up speed as it went. It even ran a red light as it slid through the center of town! It finally stopped at the front door of the drugstore when it hit the curb. When it did, the lid popped open, the old man sat up and said to the pharmacist, "Do you have anything in there to stop this coffin?"

* * *

There was this gal who thought living out in the country was no good for such an ambitious and talented person like herself. So, against her family's wishes, she left home to look for a job in the big city. "I'll show you that the big city is better than the country any day!" she said when she left. Well, she found a good job the first day she was in the city and a month later she wired home, "Thing's are much better here like I told you. Already made supervisor. Feather in my cap!" A few weeks later she wired home again, "Already made manager. I told you things were better here in the big city. Feather in my cap!" Then a few weeks after that, her family got another wire that said, "Fired from my job. Send money for ticket to come home." Her family wired back, "No ticket necessary—use your feathers to fly."

* * *

There were these two old hillbillies that had lived up in the mountains all their lives. One day while walking in to town, they met a Catholic priest whose arm was in a sling. One of the hillbillies said, "Hey priest, what happened to your arm?" He said, "Well, I slipped and fell in the bathtub," and went on his way. After the hillbillies walked down the road a ways, the one said to the other, "What's a bathtub anyway?" The other said, "How should I know? I ain't a Catholic!"

＊ ＊ ＊

Late one evening, an old country woman accidentally swallowed a watch. The next day she went to the town doctor's office and told him, "Doc, I swallowed a watch yesterday!" The doctor asked, "Well, why'd you wait until today to come and see me?" She replied, "It was too late to call you, so I thought I could just eat some prunes to pass the time."

＊ ＊ ＊

Back at the country store, the store clerk had been instructed by the owner to help enforce the new "No Smoking" ordinance. That afternoon, a man walked in enjoying a smoke. "Sir, I'm sorry, but you'll have to put out your cigarette, " the clerk requested. The customer said, "Well, you sell them in this store don't you?" The clerk said, "Yes, but we also sell Ex-Lax, and you don't see anyone in here enjoying that, do you?"

＊ ＊ ＊

There was this man back home who went to tour a big city brewery for the first time. He was from the country and had never been to a big brewery before, and while he was standing over a big vat of beer, he slipped and fell in and drowned! When the brewery called his wife and told her what had happened, she said, "Did he suffer much before he died?" The man from the brewery said, "No. In fact he climbed out three times to use the restroom before he drowned!"

＊ ＊ ＊

The town drunk was in the local bar one Saturday afternoon, and like usual, he had too many drinks. The bartender told him, "If you don't stop drinking so much you're gonna go blind!" "There's nothing wrong with my eyesight!" replied the drunk. "I'll prove it to you. Can't you see that old one-eyed cat coming in the door?" "Pardon me," the bartender replied, "but that one-eyed cat is going *out* the door."

* * *

A man from the big city was riding in the country for the first time. Out of nowhere, a big billygoat ran out in front of him, and he ran over it with his car! Well the man was shocked and confused all at the same time because he didn't know what it was. So he jumped back in his car and raced down the road until he got to a little country store. He ran in hysterically yelling, "Help! I just ran over something down the road and I don't know what it is!" The storekeeper said, "Describe it to me." The man said, "Well it's got a hard head, a big stomach, and it's about the ugliest creature I've ever seen!" The storekeeper thought about it a little, scratched his head, and then all of a sudden an old man sitting in the store jumped up and said, "Oh Lordy! You ran over my wife!"

* * *

A woman who had lived way out in the country her whole life went into town to see if she could get a loan to build a bathroom inside her house. She had never been in a bank before, so she was pretty nervous, but she got right to the point with the bank president. "I want to borrow a thousand dollars to put a bathroom in my house!" she said. The president was cautious and responded, "Well, I don't believe I know you. Do you mind telling me where you've done your business before?" She said, "Oh, out back in the woods!"

* * *

There was an out-of-town stranger passing through in his expensive sports car when he came upon a creek in the middle of the road. Sitting nearby was a farmer, so he asked him how deep the creek was. The farmer replied, "Oh, not too deep." So the stranger proceeded to drive his car straight into the creek and was surprised when all of a sudden he was in up over his roof! When he swam to shore and watched his sports car sink, he yelled at the farmer, "I thought you said this creek wasn't very deep." The farmer pointed to his chin and said, "That's funny, it only comes up to here on my duck!"

* * *

There was an old barn burning out of control with flames everywhere. The fire was so intense that it threatened to burn down the farmhouse and set the nearby woods on fire too! There were three fire companies that had already reached the scene but couldn't put out the fire. From a distance the firefighters could hear bells clanging and sirens wailing until finally a small fire truck appeared on the road. The little truck drove straight up the driveway and right into the burning barn, which extinguished the flames instantly! Three months later on the steps of city hall, the small community honored the best fire company of the year. They of course picked the small fire company with the little fire truck. When they presented the check for a thousand dollars to the fire chief the mayor asked, "So what are you going to do with the money, chief?" The chief replied, "Well, the first thing we're doing is getting those darned brakes fixed!"

* * *

Way up in the mountains in a tiny little town, an old mountaineer and his young wife were getting a divorce in the local court. The two of them were arguing feverishly over custody of their children. The mother jumped to her feet and protested to the judge, "Since I brought the children into the world, I should get to keep 'em!" Since the old mountain man also wanted custody of the kids, the judge asked for his side of the story. After a long moment of silence, the man slowly rose from his chair and said, "Judge, when I put a quarter in a candy machine and a candy bar comes out, does it belong to me or the machine?"

* * *

Back home there was an old fisherman named Henry, and every day he'd come off the lake with buckets full of fish. The surprising thing was that he only used a net to land them. One day the warden asked, "Henry, how do you always catch so many fish? You use no tackle, no rod, no reel, and no bait!"

Henry said, "Well Sir, be here tomorrow at 6 A.M. and I'll take you out with me."

The next morning they met down at the lake and set out in the boat. When they got out to the middle, Henry reached under his seat, pulled out a stick of dynamite, lit it, and threw it in the water. Within seconds after it exploded, all the fish floated to the surface and Henry scooped them up with his net and put them in his bucket.

Well the warden stood up and yelled, "Henry, you can't do that! It's illegal!" Just then Henry lit another stick of dynamite, handed it to the warden, and said, "Are you gonna talk or fish?"

* * *

A farmer and his wife were resting on the front porch after a hard days work when all of a sudden a rooster came flying around the house chasing a feisty little hen. The farmer's wife yelled, "You'd better catch those chickens and put 'em back in the coop!" The farmer smiled and said, "They'll be back," and he threw out a handful of corn. Sure enough they came back around. The rooster was still chasing the hen. The hen ran right through the corn and on around the house, but the rooster stopped to eat. The old farmer turned to his wife and said, "Honey, don't *ever* let me get that hungry."

* * *

A discouraged fisherman fished all day and didn't have a single bite. Tired, flustered, and frustrated, he started his motor and headed back to shore. All at once he heard a loud thump in the boat. He turned around and looked back and saw a huge bass lying in the bottom of the boat! He stopped, reached back, grabbed the bass, and threw it back into the water! He yelled, "You didn't want to get in my boat all day so don't think you can get a free ride now!"

* * *

A old country farmer went in to town to talk to the local air conditioning man. "I need an estimate to air condition my chicken coop," he said. "I've noticed the hens lay more eggs in cool weather." "I see," the salesman nodded. "While I'm out there, would you like an estimate on the house too?" "Nah," the farmer answered, "my wife don't lay eggs."

* * *

A man with a rickety wagon and a more rickety looking horse stopped in front of the local bar. As the bartender served up a beer to the man he said, "That horse of yours don't seem to feel very good. I don't think I've ever seen such a wobbly creature!" "Oh, he's alright. He's just having a streak of bad luck," said the man. "You see, I flip a coin every morning to see if I buy some hay for the horse or a beer for me, and the horse has lost the last ten days straight!"

* * *

There were three men riding in a pickup truck on their way to the lake to do some ice fishing. Since there was only room for two of them in the cab, the third was forced to ride outside in the open box. As they were driving on the ice to their shanty, the truck broke through and sank to the bottom! The two men in the cab were able to open up the windows, swim out and up to the hole made on the top of the ice. Shivering from the cold, they were worried about their friend who had been riding in the back. After a long delay, the third man finally popped up to the surface. The other two men were pretty surprised that he was under for so long and asked, "What took you so long?" The third man answered, "Well, I had some trouble getting the tailgate down."

* * *

It seems this fellow was out in the woods hunting for deer as he usually did each year. While he was on watch, a group of wild turkeys came by. Now turkeys were out of season, but the man couldn't resist the temptation and he managed to shoot three. As luck would have it, just then a deer came along and he bagged it too. After cleaning out the deer he shoved the

Courtesy of Bill Turner

Almost every Friday after joining Ralph Emery for his live show on TNN, Henry Cannon would drive Minnie across the lot to "be with the 'King'," Roy Acuff, on the Grand Ole Opry.

turkeys inside it so no one would see them. As he started to drag the deer from the woods, a game warden stopped him, checked his tag and the deer, saw that everything seemed to be in order, and offered to help the man drag the heavy deer out of the woods. The man said, "Oh no, I can do it myself!" But the officer insisted and off they went.

Well after a short time, the three turkeys came tumbling out and the officer looked the hunter straight in the eye and said, "Well, what do you have to say for yourself?" The man sheepishly looked down at the turkeys and then at the warden and replied, "Boy, good thing I shot that deer. He would've eaten the whole flock!"

✳ ✳ ✳

A husband and wife were traveling cross country and they were arguing about how to pronounce the name of the small town that they were in. They decided that the best way to settle the argument was to ask someone who lived there. So they stopped at a restaurant and gave their order to the waitress. When the waitress returned with their food, the wife asked, "Would you please tell us where we are and be sure to say it real slow." The waitress leaned over and said, "D-A-I-R-Y Q-U-E-E-N!"

* * *

A Texas farmer was visiting an Australian farm for the first time. He asked, "What's that growing out there in that field?" His Aussie host answered, "Them are watermelons, mate." The Texan scoffed and said, "In Texas, we grow potatoes bigger than that! What's that over there on those trees?" The Aussie farmer replied, "Those are our finest Australian apples." The Texan said, "In Texas, we grow grapes bigger than that!"

Just then, three kangaroos hopped by at a furious pace. The startled Texan asked, "What were those?" The Australian farmer replied, "You mean you don't have grasshoppers in Texas?"

* * *

Up in the northern frontiers of North America, two mountain men were taking their first flight, flying from the west coast to the east coast in a four engine plane. As they were flying over a vast wilderness, there was nothing but mountains and forests below them. After flying for a little while they heard a bang after which the pilot came out and said, "Nothing to worry about. We've lost one engine but that just means it will take an extra hour to get where we're going." A while later the same thing happened and the pilot came out and said, "No need to worry. Another engine quit but it just means it'll take us two extra hours." An hour later a third engine quit to which the pilot said it would now take them three hours extra. After hearing that, one of the mountain men said to the other, "I sure hope that fourth engine don't quit or we'll be up here all day!"

16.
The Wild Kingdom

There's a certain scents-ability that comes with living in the country. You quickly come to know what part of town to be in depending on which way the wind is wafting. Nature is truly a magnificent beauty to behold except when you're be-holding your nose to appreciate it. If you live someplace like Grinder's Switch, you're sure to get your fill of the wild kingdom. There are dogs beneath every stoop, cattle lowing, pigs oinking, and chickens clucking on farms, and it's almost inevitable that you'll spy a flock of turkeys gobbling in the straw piles. I'm excluding, of course, the gaggle of men who roost down at the Switch before the morning express.

I did mention dogs, didn't I? Yes, I did. I'm afraid that if a man was put to the test of choosing between his mate or his hunting hound, the latter would always get a sure date for a Saturday walk in the woods. After all, they are man's best friend. But a dog has to grow into this state of grace and bonding with his master because no country gentleman worth his salt would ever admit that his prize canine was once a floundering pup.

You see, that's where the womenfolk are an integral part of the master plan. Puppies by nature are cute, and the ladies adore comely things. Why just the thought of a man's prize setter once shrouded in a pink sweater, lovingly crocheted with a nice cotton blend at the last gentlewomen's social is enough to drive a "feller" to the sauce. In spite of this, however, and with the proper ration of table scraps and as few soap baths from Mammy as possible, there's hope that a faithful dog like Minnie's pooch, Careless, is bound to evolve.

Now if you happen to speak in earthly terms that pertain to creatures outside of this small circle of beastly evolution, like elephants and hippopotami, then you might be on your own way out in rural America. You see, if you live far enough out in the country it's generally a pretty far bus ride to the nearest city zoo. Most folks would likely prefer to content themselves by listening to the bullfrogs and swatting horse-flies than to spend money on the round-trip city express and zoo fare. To quote some old wives, "The finer things in life *are* free," and "What you don't know won't hurt you." Unless of course it's a two-thousand-pound elephant escaped from the traveling circus.

✳ ✳ ✳

A circus train pulled into a railroad siding on the outskirts of a small town. While unloading, an elephant escaped and made its way to a nearby farm. The farmer's wife, alone at the time, had never seen an elephant before. When she looked out the window and saw the huge animal she immediately called the sheriff. "Sheriff," she said, "there's a huge animal that I've never seen before in my cabbage patch!" "What does it look like?" the sheriff asked. She replied. "It's about ten feet tall, has four legs, and two tails. I can't tell front from back. It's got one small tail on one end and a big long tail on the other end." "Well, what's it doing?" the sheriff asked. "It's pulling up my cabbages with its long tail," she replied. "What's it doing with the cabbages?" asked the sheriff. She replied, "Sheriff, you wouldn't believe me if I told you!"

✳ ✳ ✳

Brother's a good boy. He's got a big bowl of goldfish at home. You know what he's done recently? He took picture postcards of New York and Florida and pasted them around the sides of the goldfish bowl. He said he seen them little old fishes swimmin' around the bowl and wanted to make 'em think they was goin' somewhere!

* * *

I was ridin' on the bus and it was awful crowded and I had never had so much trouble in my life. All of a sudden the bus run into somethin'. The bus run over this little old dog and cut his tail off. Just plum whacked it off! It didn't hurt his carriage much, but it sure played willy with his waggin'!

I jumped out of that bus and grabbed that little old dog and his tail up and run over to a tailor store where they make britches and things. I asked the man if he could sew the little dog's tail back on. And he said, "No! The law would get me for re-tailin' dogs without a license!"

* * *

Old Uncle Nabob started raising goats a couple of weeks ago, but he tried to keep it a secret from all the neighbors. Somehow they got wind of it.

* * *

I had an awful hard time getting to town today. I like to not made it. We was gettin' ready to get on the bus down there at Grinder's Switch, and the bus stopped and me and Mammy and Brother and Sister and Aunt Ambrosia and Uncle Nabob and our old dog Careless was gonna get on. And everybody got on except Careless, that old dog. The bus driver said, "No! That dog can't get on the bus!" I said, "Careless has got to get on the bus. He's got to go with us. He's just like a member of the family!" The bus driver said, "I can see the family resemblance, but he still don't ride this bus!"

* * *

Up in Grinder's Switch, Old Moonshine McGinny's got him a brand new dog and he's learnin' him some new tricks. Why he's got that dog trained so that he goes around and puts stoppers in all his jugs! When I asked him what kind of a dog it was, Old Moonshine said, "He's a Corker Spaniel!"

* * *

Uncle Nabob's got him a new business. He's raising fleas for a New York flea circus. That's one business that's definitely got to start from scratch, ain't it? When I asked him how was his business doin', he said, "Not so good. The flea business has gone to the dogs."

Well, Brother's got these three old trick dogs. He's all the time tryin' to learn 'em to do tricks, you know. Well, the other day he was tryin' to teach 'em a new trick. He snapped his fingers and one little ol' dog turned a flip and landed on his feet. I said, "That ain't so hard. I seen that done before." He snapped his fingers again and the second little dog turned a flip and landed on top of the other little dog. I said, "That ain't so hard either. I seen that done before." Well, he snapped his fingers and the third little dog turned a flip, and landed on top of those other two little dogs, and started singin' the "Yankee Doodle!" This man that was lookin' on said, "Now that's incredible! I want to buy that top dog!" Brother said, "No you don't. You want the middle dog. He's a ventriloquist and he's throwin' his voice!"

* * *

Once upon a time, a long time ago when the beasts could talk, the Lion thought he would go out among the other animals and speak to them. So he set out, and the first animal he came across was the Monkey. Now, the Lion is a large beast, and he is ferocious, so he intimidated other animals. He scowled fiercely, and asked the Monkey, "Who's the king of the jungle?" The Monkey chittered and chattered and finally said, "You are! The mighty Lion!" This pleased the Lion, and he went on his way.

Then, he met the Hyena. Again he roared, "Who is the king of the jungle?" And the Hyena, being a coward anyway, said, "Why you are, O mighty Lion!" This made the Lion more pleased than ever, so he went happily on his way. All through the jungle he went, asking his question and getting the same reply.

Finally, he came to the Elephant. He roared out his question, and the Elephant reached out with his trunk, grabbed the

Lion by the tail and swung him around and around his head, and then let the Lion go tossing him into a bush! When the Lion got his breath back he walked up to the Elephant and said, "Well just because you don't know the answer is no reason to get mad!"

* * *

There was once a man from the city who was visiting a farm. During his visit he saw a farmer feeding pigs. The farmer would lift the pig up to a nearby apple tree and the pig would eat the apples off of the tree. The farmer would move the pig from one apple to another until the pig was satisfied and then he would start with the next pig.

The city man watched this for some time with great astonishment. Finally, he couldn't resist and walked up to the farmer and said, "Just think of the time that you'd save if you simply shook the apples off of the tree and let the pigs eat them off of the ground!"

The farmer looked puzzled and asked, "What's time to a pig?"

* * *

A country minister had just enjoyed a hearty chicken dinner at the home of one of one of his parishioners. Gazing out of the window he noticed a rooster and remarked, "That rooster sure seems to be a mighty proud and happy bird!"

His host replied, "Well he should! His oldest son just entered the ministry!"

* * *

Farmer Brown phoned the old town veterinarian and said he had a sick cat. "The cat just lays around all day and whines," he told the vet. The old doctor said, "That's nothing. Give him a pint of castor oil." So, the farmer did, and a few days later he met the vet in town. "How's that sick calf?" asked the doctor. "Calf? It wasn't a *calf*, it was a sick *cat!*" explained Farmer Brown. "Goodness gracious," exclaimed the vet! "Did you give the cat a whole pint of castor oil?" "Yep," said the farmer.

"Well, what did he do?" asked the old doctor. Farmer Brown said, "Last I seen him, he was going over the hill with five other cats. Two were diggin', two were covering up, and one was scouting for more ground!"

* * *

Some tourists from the big city were driving through a quaint old country town when they noticed a field full of cows and a farmer who was taking all of the round bales of hay, loading them onto a wagon, and driving them away. Curious as to why the farmer was taking away the cows' food, they stopped and asked him about it. He said, "Well, the county agent came by here and told us to pick 'em all up. He said the cows weren't getting a square meal!"

* * *

A traveling salesman became lost way out in the country. While driving down a dirt road, he spied a house with a farmer in the yard. He pulled his car up to the farmer and asked him for directions back to town. While the farmer was giving the salesman directions, the salesman couldn't help but notice a pig pen with a large hog inside. To his surprise, the hog had a wooden peg in place of his right hind leg.

After receiving directions to town, the salesman asked about the hog's wooden leg. The farmer replied, "That's not just any hog. That's a special hog. Why last summer I was plowing in that field over there and the tractor turned over on me, pinning me under it! Well sir, that hog saw what happened, rooted under the fence, and ran out to where I was. Then he rooted all around me 'til I could crawl out from under the tractor! Yes sir, that hog saved my life!" The salesman said the hog was indeed special, but it still didn't explain the wooden peg in place of his right hind leg. "Son," the farmer said looking at the hog, "with a hog as special as he is, you don't want to eat it all at once!"

* * *

This couple was going to give a dinner party. The menu consisted of salad and steak with mushrooms. When it came time to cook, they discovered they had no mushrooms. "That's okay," said the husband. "I'll go out to the woods and pick some wild ones." "How will we know if they're poisonous?" asked his wife. "Well, we'll feed some to the dog first," answered her husband. So they did as planned and the dog liked them and all seemed to be fine.

Their guests arrived, and they ate heartily until one of the guests came back into the dining room and announced that while he was outside he witnessed the death of the family dog!

Well, the two hosts panicked and immediately rushed their friends to the hospital to have their stomachs pumped. After the ordeal, the hosts asked the one guest, "Did the dog have to suffer very long?" The guest replied, "No. The truck that hit him killed him instantly!"

* * *

A man was driving down the highway with four penguins in the backseat of his car. Seeing this little spectacle, a policeman stopped him and said, "You know it's against the law to drive with animals in your car." The man explained, "I'm just taking them to the zoo." The policeman believed him and told him to be on his way.

The next day the policeman saw the man again with the penguins still in his backseat, except this time they were each wearing a pair of sunglasses. The policeman said, "I thought you said yesterday you were taking those penguins to the zoo?" The man replied, "Well officer, yesterday I took them to the zoo. Today, I'm taking them to the beach!"

* * *

A farmer was checking his new farm animals to see if they were male or female. He would pick one up and look under and say, "This is a male," then pick up another and look under and say, "This is a female." His little nephew who was visiting the farm for the first time asked his cousin how his dad could tell just by

It isn't uncommon for legends to gather together for performances of the Grand Ole Opry as seen here (left to right) when Hank Snow, Ernest Tubb, Minnie, Hal Durham and Roy Acuff celebrated the Opry's 55th birthday in 1980.

looking under the animal if it was a boy or girl. His cousin said, "I don't know. I guess it's printed on the bottom."

* * *

A mountain boy was late for school one morning claiming that he was tardy because he was cleaning chickens. The principal didn't think his excuse was adequate and asked for an explanation. The boy said, "Well, Maw woke up Pa at three o'clock in the morning because she heard a noise in the henhouse. So Pa didn't take time to get dressed, grabbed his shotgun and ran outside. He pointed it straight at the henhouse and waited for something to happen. Just then our old hound dog snuck up behind Pa with his cold nose and bam! We've been cleaning chickens ever since."

* * *

A lady, traveling alone, was taking a long plane trip to where she and her husband both grew up. Upon arriving at the airport she informed the airline that she wanted to take her dog with her in the cabin. She became very angry when the airline told her she couldn't, but finally gave in and allowed them to put the dog in the baggage compartment. The manager said, "It will be warm and pressurized in there, and your dog should be fine." Upon arrival at the first fuel stop, the crew went to check on the dog and found it dead! The airline crew quickly ran all over town until they found a dog of the same color, height, weight, and sex and put it in the cage.

Upon arrival at their final destination they hand delivered the lady her dog. Quite surprised the woman said, "That's not my dog!" The airline manager said, "Sure it's your dog. Look! It's the same height, weight, color, and sex as when we loaded it." The lady again insisted, "That's not my dog!" The manager asked her, "Just how do you know that this isn't your dog?" She answered, "Because my dog was dead! I was taking it home to bury it next to my husband!"

* * *

Little Jenny was visiting her grandmother on the farm for the first time. One day she spotted a peacock, a bird she had never seen before. She stared at it silently for a few moments, then ran into the house crying, "Oh Granny, come look quick! One of your chickens is blooming!"

* * *

A man had a pet rat that he had taught how to talk. He also taught the rat how to drink liquor. Whenever he went out he would carry the rat in his coat pocket. One day he went into a bar and ordered two drinks. He drank one and slowly poured the other drink into his coat pocket. The bartender seeing this decided not to let him have any more to drink.

When the man asked for two more drinks the bartender said, "I'm sorry, fella. You've already had enough!" The man said, "I've only had one drink! I want to see the manager! Get him out here! Just then the rat stuck his head up out of the man's coat pocket and said. "Yeah! And tell him to bring his stupid cat with him too!"

* * *

Do you know why the cowboy bought a basset hound? Everyone told him to "get a-long little doggie!"

* * *

There was this gambler who spent a lot of time and money betting on dogs. He loved the races more than anything. One day he bet his life savings on a greyhound that looked to be a terrific favorite and was named Speedy. Unfortunately, he had placed his bet before he found out about the dog's one bad habit. Whenever he got to the last turn, he would veer to the left, hit the rail and lose the race even though he had led it from the start. The gambler who bet on him was thoroughly disgusted and thought he had a solution that would keep Speedy from hitting the fence. So he found the dog's owner. "His veering left might have to do with his balance," the gambler said. "Why not put a small piece of lead in his right ear." "That's a great idea," the dog's owner said, "but what do I use to put the lead in?" The gambler said, "Why not try a pistol."

* * *

There was this hunter who was proud of his retriever because the dog who could walk on top of the lake water. No one believed it was true, so he invited a friend to witness the dog's ability. As the hunter shot a duck over the lake the retriever jumped out of the boat, walked over the water, and brought the duck back. The friend observed, but said nothing. A little later on, the hunter shot down a second duck, and just like the first time, the dog jumped out of the boat, walked on top of the water, and brought the duck back to the boat. The friend *still* didn't comment. After he shot down a third duck and the same performance was repeated by the retriever, the hunter became annoyed over his friend's silence and so he asked, "Didn't you notice anything when I shot down those three ducks?" His friend said, "Yeah. That fool dog can't swim."

* * *

There were two rabbits grazing in the valley when suddenly a pack of hungry wolves appeared. The first rabbit said, "Should we make a run for it or stay here and outnumber them?" The second rabbit said, "Run for your life, dummy! Remember, we're *brothers*!"

* * *

A talent scout had advertised auditions for animal acts to be on a television show. So a man and his dog appeared at the audition and he explained to the scout that his dog could talk. The talent scout was skeptical, but told him to show him the dog's talents anyway. First, the man asked the dog, "What's on the outside of a tree?" "Bark! Bark!" said the dog. "Good boy," he said. "What's on the top of a house?" "Roof! Roof!" the dog said. At this point the talent scout was becoming a little exasperated. "Okay! Who was the greatest baseball player of all time?" the man asked the dog. "Ruth! Ruth!" the dog replied. "Alright. That's enough! Get out of here," the talent scout yelled. "Any dog can make those sounds!" So as the man and his dog were leaving the audition, the dog turned and said to his master, "I guess I should have said DiMaggio instead."

* * *

An eagle lost his mate. He went looking for another and found a dove, took it home, and the dove kept saying, "I am dove and want to make love." He got tired of the dove, so he went out looking again. This time he found a loon and took him home. The loon kept saying, "I am loon and want to spoon." He got tired of the loon, so he went looking again. This time he found a duck and took him home and the duck said, "I'm a drake and you made a mistake."

* * *

One day a traveling salesman went up to the gate at a man's house. When he did, a dog started barking at him. The man appeared on the porch so the salesman asked him, "Will your dog bite?" The man said, "Nope. My dog doesn't bite." So, the salesman opened the gate, and walked in and just as he did the dog bit him.

The salesman yelled, "I thought you said your dog wouldn't bite!" The man answered, "I did, but that's not my dog!"

* * *

Once a family had a big beautiful dog. Well, it was a good dog except for one thing. It always gave the neighbor's pet rabbit the evil eye. When the neighbors with the rabbit went on vacation, the family noticed their dog out in the neighbor's yard pawing at the ground and then with the rabbit in its mouth shaking it for all it was worth! Not knowing exactly what to do, the owners of the dog devised a plan. They took the rabbit, gave it a bath, blow dried its fur, and stuck it back in its cage. When the rabbit's owners came home they said to the dog's owner, "It's strange, but before we left, our rabbit died and we buried it, and for the life of us we can't figure out how it got back in its cage."

* * *

Sam the Tomcat was scurrying all over the neighborhood. Down the alleys, up the fire escapes, down stairways, and hurrying into cellars. A concerned friend and neighbor knocked on the owner's door and said, "Your cat is running all over the neighborhood as if he were mad!"

"I know," the owner replied. "We just had him 'fixed' and he's been running around canceling engagements."

* * *

Two young career girls were going home after a long day at work. One of the girls stopped, bent down, and picked up a frog from the grass beside the walk. She asked, "Frog, did you just talk to me?" The frog responded, "Yes, I did. A wicked witch cast a spell on me and turned me into a frog and the only way I can become a handsome young man again is to be kissed by a beautiful young lady. I'm not only a handsome young man, but I also am a big landowner and if you give me a kiss and I return to normal, I'll give you a five-hundred-acre farm!"

The girl promptly popped the frog into her purse and continued on her way home. Her friend looked puzzled and asked, "Aren't you going to kiss the frog?" The girl replied, "Are you kidding? Considering the money farmers earn today, I'll make more money with a talking frog!"

Courtesy of David Skepner

It was rare to catch Sarah Cannon's (a.k.a. Minnie Pearl) husband, Henry, on film and equally as rare to capture Loretta Lynn's husband, Mooney. They're seen here together (from left to right: Mooney Lynn, Sarah Cannon, Loretta's manager, David Skepner, Loretta Lynn, and Henry Cannon.)

17.
Do Drop In

Minnie Pearl had so many friends it would be impossible to include them all in one book. And I think all of her fans consider themselves to be friends in a way too and would be insulted if they weren't included. So like it happens in the country, a handful of folks are dropping in here to say a few things about Minnie. Some are involved in management, some are business people, but all are friends.

One of those folks is Marion Howard. Marion worked for Minnie eleven years, first managing the Minnie Pearl Museum and Gift Shop, and then as personal secretary. She told me that there were many wonderful stories that she used to hear. I decided to include this one about Brother.

> Some people in Grinder's Switch thought that Brother wasn't wrapped too tight and that he might not be dealing with all fifty-two cards, if you know what I mean. Truth is, he had an exceptional short-term memory. In fact, it was so exceptionally short that he couldn't remember things from one minute to the next. You see, one day a feller was goin' down the road and saw Brother standing on the side with a bridle in his hand. He asked, "Hey Brother, what have you got there?" Brother looked kind of perplexed and said, "Well, I'm not sure if I found a bridle or lost a horse."

Bob Whitaker, who was entertainment director for the Opryland Theme Park and manager for the Grand Ole Opry, recalled Minnie with great love. "She was a great lady. When I was working for Opryland, we had young people portray Minnie Pearl, and we wanted Minnie to bless that character. So we would call her every time we had an audition, and she loved that. Afterwards, she would invite these young folks out to her house and talk to them for hours and explain to these aspiring entertainers the importance of performing. She'd tell them, 'You're not out there for you. You're there for the audience. Never forget your audience. Just love 'em and they'll love you back.' And I know that she really meant that." He also remembered the days when Minnie would sit in front of the Acuff Theater at Opryland in a rocking chair with dozens of the theme park's dancers and singers gathered around listening to her.

He also reminisced that when Minnie would arrive at the Opry there was always a buzz. He said, "It was magic! Electric! You knew that she was here! It didn't matter where she was, she was always a magnet, whether she was Minnie Pearl or Sarah Cannon." Bob said he never saw her when she didn't seem to enjoy being Minnie Pearl.

Another friend, David Skepner, who has managed stars like Loretta Lynn and Riders in the Sky, teaches music business courses at Belmont University in Nashville where he confessed, "She brought me cake for fifteen years." He recalled a story that she would always tell at his class. It had to do with when she was first traveling on the Opry. It wasn't like it is nowadays. There weren't huge fleets of tour busses. Some of the biggest stars of the Opry at that time traveled together from show to show in a station wagon. One rainy Sunday afternoon for a matinee there were about eight people in the audience. So Minnie decided that she would play her entire show to the band, hardly paying attention to the small crowd. Only afterwards did she find out that there was a Broadway producer there that day considering her to be leading actress for a part in a new musical, *Oklahoma*. Needless to say, she didn't get the part. "That's one of life's lessons. Always do your best," she told every class.

I would be remiss if I didn't include the producer of the *Nashville Now* program while I was there. Bill Turner was the man responsible for giving me my first job in Music City. As I

Television and Silver Screen legend, George Burns, and Minnie Pearl share a moment backstage at the Grand Ole Opry House.

Courtesy of Les Leverett

mentioned early on, he was also the one who let me get away with as much as I did while I was a writer on the show. Most important, he was very good about introducing me to country music's "Who's Who." This, of course, included Minnie Pearl. When I asked Bill about some of his favorite Minnie jokes, he reminded me of two that I had somehow overlooked. Both take place at a retirement home, but they still have a lot of get up and go when it comes to laughter.

> A forgetful old man was talking to a lady friend whom he had just met the day before at their retirement home, and she was bragging about how sharp her mind still was. The man wasn't convinced, so she said to him, "I'll prove to you that my mind is in tip-top shape." The man said, "How?" She answered, "Take off all of your clothes and I'll tell you how old you are." The man said, "You're on!" and he stripped down naked right on the front porch. He said, "OK, smartypants. How old am I?" She replied, "You're going to turn seventy-eight in two

weeks on the eighth!" The man was amazed and said, "You're exactly right! How did you know?" She answered, "You told me yesterday, you old goat!"

I guess the mind goes first and then the eyes...

Two old gentlemen were sitting in the living room at their retirement home when an old woman resident went running down the hallway without a stitch of clothing on. The two men looked at each other and one said to the other, "Who was that who just went by?" The other answered, "I don't know who, but whatever she was wearing sure needed ironing!"

As for me, every moment and conversation with Minnie is a cherished memory. Unfortunately, I haven't been holding out on you. I've put every one of my favorite jokes and stories of hers in this book already. That is, unless of course my memory gets jostled somewhere down the road and more fall out.

Minnie Pearl was in a class all her own. Her character and stage presence were such that you can't easily pigeonhole her into a single category. Such is the case with a lot of jokes and stories too. And I think as you read the rest of this collection, you'll find that the tales included defy being classified too!

18.
A Little of This and That (from the General Store of Humor)

If you come from Grinder's Switch or even from the big city, you're doubtless all too familiar with a "pot luck dinner." If not, that's when you take the "pullings" off Sunday's hen, stir it in a pot with Monday's leftover roast, line some Pyrex with Tuesday's extra cornbread, pour in just a touch of Wednesday's noodles a la grandma, add a pinch of Thursday's grits for texture, and top it off with a hunk of Friday's flounder, and you've got "Pot Luck Saturday." Then, I think by law, the gastronomic cycle begins again.

Well, we've reached that point in this journal too. Because as sure as the world turns and the sun rises in the East and sets in the West, there are some narratives that demand their own category. Tales that reject affiliation with other themes. Maybe they just stand out in a crowd. Much to the dismay of the perpetrators of such storytelling, I've gathered those "pot luck leftovers" under the "miscellaneous" classification.

This doesn't mean that they aren't worthy of special praise. Heavens no! There are truly some jewels in this pile of rubble. So it's time for you to break out the "Horn of Plenty" and fill it with this potpourri of funny business.

* * *

A bunch of us from Grinder's Switch were going up to New York City. Someone asked me, "Suppose some city slicker up there in New York tries to come along and sell you the Brooklyn Bridge. Would you buy it?" I told 'em, "Don't be silly. I know the Brooklyn Bridge ain't for sale. Everybody in town knows that Uncle Nabob bought it ten years ago! He traded a feller a sack of cockleburs and told him they was porcupine eggs." They asked me, "Well, has Brother ever tried to sell it?" I told 'em, "No. He says he's keepin' it for an investment. He said it's sort of like milkin' a cow. You have to hold on to it for a long pull."

Someone asked when I was up there was I gonna wear one of those strapless, backless evening gowns those pretty girls up there wear. I told 'em, "Oh no! Mammy wouldn't let me do that. None of them strapless, backless things for me." I said, "Did you ever notice that when the girls wear those low-cut strapless things they're all sittin' down? You know why that is? It's 'cause they're afraid if they stand up the dress won't get up when they do!"

Uncle Nabob had a big time when we was up there. He said that town is full of precious metal. You can pick it up all over the streets. Right when he got off the streetcar he picked up a silver dollar. Then he went about a block and picked up a gold pin. He went about two more blocks and picked up a platinum blonde.

* * *

You know, this past week we had us a wild wind up there in Grinder's Switch. You know, with March comin' in like a lion. Well, I want you to know that one day that strong wind just picked my brother up, right up in the air, and landed him over in Smiley Dillard's haystack. It wouldn't have been so bad, but he landed right straight on a pitchfork! Brother said he didn't mind the takeoff so much, but oooh! That three-point landing!

* * *

Back in Grinder's Switch, there was a time I took voice lessons. And my voice teacher once said I had a voice like a thrush! A nightingale! A mockingbird! My boyfriend Hezzie said, "He told you that?" I said, "Well, not in so many words. What he said exactly was, 'Minnie, that voice of yours is strictly for the birds!' "

* * *

We had an awful fog the other night at Grinder's Switch. It was just so dark and foggy and Lucifer Hucklehead was out in his car. He couldn't have stayed on the road at all if he hadn't kept following the taillights on the car in front of him. When that car would turn left, Lucifer would turn left. When the car would turn right, Lucifer would turn right. All of a sudden the car stopped quick and Lucifer run smack dab into the back end of it! Lucifer hollered out, "Hey, you're supposed to stick out your hand when you stop!" And the feller in the car said, "Oh yeah? Even when I stop in my own garage?"

* * *

I'm so proud of my brother. He's so handsome. That runs in our family. It done run out by the time it got to me! And I love the way that Brother wears his teeth, you know. Parted in the middle.

He was supposed to come to town with us today. We all got ready to leave this morning up there at the Switch. And everybody's all loaded in the barouche, and we waited for Brother. We waited about an hour. So I finally decided to go and get Brother. He's forgetful, you know. He'll just sit and think, and sometimes just sit. I went over to Brother's room and there he was just sittin' there lookin' at himself in the mirror. He'd been sittin' there all morning tryin' to remember where he'd seen himself before!

* * *

I was walkin' down the street today and there was two nice looking fellers just standing there, and I looked over and smiled and they looked over at me and laughed out loud. One of them said to the other, "Ain't that the ugliest girl you've ever seen?" The other one said, "Yeah, she's ugly, but she may be a pretty good old girl. You know beauty's only skin deep." The other one said, "Well, let's skin her!"

I don't know what to say to fellers. I ain't never been around much. Except that time I went into town and leaned over to tie my shoe and got caught in a revolvin' door. I made three hundred round trips in that thing before I could get out! It scared Mammy to death. She kept on sayin', "Speak to me, Minnie! Speak to me, Minnie!" And I did, every time I came around. "Howdy, Mammy! Howdy, Mammy! Howdy, Mammy!"

* * *

Brother took Hezzie's car out last week and got it all banged up. He was out drivin' on the highway, and it turns out he was drivin' on the wrong side of the road. I said to him, "Brother, don't you ever see that white line down the highway? That's the guide. *You* stay on the right side, and the people goin' in the opposite direction stay on the other side of it." And Brother was so surprised! He said, "I always thought that white line was for bicycles!"

* * *

Fall weather in Grinder's Switch is just grand. It reminds me of Uncle Nabob taking his jug on a plane trip. He always likes a little nip in the air!

* * *

Three men were walking on the beach when one of them stumbled on something. Seeing that it was an old brass lamp, one picked it up, rubbed some sand off, and to their surprise a beautiful genie came out! The genie said, "For freeing me from the lamp, I will grant one wish to each of you." So, the first man wished, "I want to be ten times smarter than I am right now!" With a nod and a puff of smoke the genie said, "You are now ten times smarter than you were."

The second man thought for a minute and said, "I want to be one hundred times smarter than I am right now!" Again, with a nod and a puff of smoke the genie said, "You are now one hundred times smarter than you were!"

When it was the third man's turn, he quickly said, "I want to be one thousand times smarter than I am right now!" The genie looked at the man, and with a nod and puff of smoke, she said, "You are now a woman!"

* * *

Back home a highway worker was given the job of painting white lines down the middle of the main road out of town. On his first day he painted six miles. The next day he painted three more miles. But the following day, he painted less than a mile. When his foreman asked him why he kept painting less each day, the worker said back, "I'm sorry, boss. I just can't do any better. Every day I keep getting farther away from the paint can!"

* * *

This man walked into a bank carrying a box, and he wanted to borrow some money. The receptionist introduced him to the loan officer, Miss Patty Wack. "Sir," said Patty Wack, "what do you have as collateral for a loan?" "Why, I've got this box," the man said. "Yes, I can see that, but what is it?" asked Miss Patty Wack. "I don't really know," he said. So Patty took the box and went back to her supervisor's office. She said, "Sir, there's a man out front who wants to borrow some money and all he has is this box for collateral, and I have no idea what it is!" The supervisor took the box, looked it over, and said, "Why that's a knickknack Patty Wack, give the man a loan!"

* * *

Two ol' army buddies ran into each other after twenty years. One asked the other, "How's your wife doing?" He said, "Well, she ran off with a vacuum salesman ten years ago!" The first said, "That's too bad. Well, how's your daughter doing?" He replied, "Well, she was so upset about her mother that she wound up in a mental institution." The first said again, "Boy! That's too bad! Well, how's your son doing?" He said, "He was so upset about his mom that he went after the vacuum salesman, and now he's serving a life sentence!" Stunned, the first man hesitated and then asked, "Well, what are you doing now?" His buddy answered, "Oh, you know, the same ol' thing. Still selling good luck charms."

* * *

As the president of the Women's Guild desperately leafed through her rolodex for a guest speaker to replace a last minute cancellation, her doorbell rang. It was two men who offered to do work around the house in return for a meal. She agreed to provide them with dinner if they chopped the wood in back of the house. Ten minutes later, she glanced out the window to see one of the men whirl across the lawn, performing a succession of double flips and one-handed cartwheels before disappearing into some bushes. Rushing out, she grabbed the second man and gushed, "That was amazing! Do you think your friend would be willing to do that again at the Women's Guild this afternoon? I'll pay him twenty dollars!" "Hey Charley!" the man yelled out. "The lady here wants to know if you'd chop off another finger for twenty bucks!"

* * *

A man was walking along a highway one very hot sunny day when he passed a sign that proclaimed he had just entered the state of Florida. A little further on he noticed a roadside stand that displayed a big sign advertising "Orange juice. All you can drink for twenty-five cents." Well, the man was pretty thirsty from walking, so he went over to the stand and plunked down his quarter and said, "I think I'll take you up on your juice deal!" The attendant filled up a big glass with cool orange juice, and the man downed it very quickly. He pushed the glass back and said, "Fill it up again!" The attendant said, "OK. That'll be twenty-five cents, please." The man replied, "But your sign says, 'All you can drink for twenty-five cents.' " The attendant looked at him and said, "That *is* all you can drink for twenty-five cents!"

* * *

An older couple had been wanting a child for a long time. Finally, they were blessed, but when the baby was born, it only had a head and no body. When it was twenty-one, the father took it down to the local tavern to celebrate. They ordered a couple of martinis. Suddenly, the head grew the complete body of a full-grown man. They were so happy that they ordered another round of drinks! When the head drank up the second drink he fell over dead. The bartender looked down at him and said, "He should have quit while he was a head."

* * *

Three women who had gone to college together but hadn't seen each other since graduation met for lunch at a swanky bistro and were doing their best to impress each other. The first lady said, "My husband bought me a necklace and earring set worth $25,000, but I had to return them because I'm allergic to platinum." The second woman added, "I understand exactly what you mean. My husband bought me a mink coat that cost $25,000, and I had to return it to the furrier because *I* was allergic to it!" Just then, the third woman fainted. When she regained consciousness the other two asked what had caused her to faint. She answered, "I guess I'm just allergic to hot air!"

* * *

Approaching a tollbooth on a busy interstate highway, traffic was backed up for miles as the result of a huge semi-truck crashing into the tollbooth. Finally, a truck drove up to the scene, a work crew jumped out, rushed up to the booth, and busily started repairing it. They applied a substance to the broken pieces, placed them back in order, and had everything put back together in no time! A motorist who had witnessed the whole operation was amazed. He got out of his car and approached one of the workmen and asked, "What on earth was that stuff you used to put the tollbooth back together so fast?" The workman replied, "Oh, that was toll gate booth paste."

* * *

A man bought a coal mine and decided he needed to hire some people to run it for him. The first man he interviewed was a big man, so he said, "I'll hire you to dig out the rocks and put them in a coal cart." The next man was a big man also, so he said, "You're strong, so you'll bring the car from the back of the mine to the front." The next man was a very small, oriental man, so he said, "Since you're not as big and strong, I'll put you in charge of supplies."

The man came back to the mine a few weeks later and found the first man digging out rocks and putting them in the cart. The second man was pushing the cart from the back of the mine to the front just as he was supposed to. Everything seemed fine until he noticed the oriental man was nowhere to be found. He asked the other men, "Where is the oriental guy?" And they said, "Oh, he's way back in the mine." So the owner walked way back in the shaft, and suddenly the oriental man jumped out yelling, "Supplies! Supplies!"

* * *

Two men were out hiking in the woods when they suddenly came upon a huge grizzly bear. Not knowing exactly what to do, the two turned and started running as fast as they could. When they turned and looked back they had made some ground on the bear, but it was obvious that it would catch up to them soon.

All of a sudden one of the two hikers stopped and started putting on some tennis shoes. His friend was hysterical and yelled, "Hurry! Why are you putting on your tennis shoes? You'll never outrun that bear!" The other said, "I don't have to outrun the bear, I just have to outrun you!"

* * *

There was a proud Indian chief named Shortcake who passed on to the great resting place in the sky. Stricken with grief, his squaw disappeared for many days. When she finally returned, the medicine man asked, "Where have you been?" She replied, "Squaw bury Shortcake."

* * *

A carpet layer worked all day laying carpet in the downstairs of a big house. Along about three o'clock he finished. But when he looked back over the room he noticed a big bulge in the center of the last room. He felt in his shirt pocket for his pack of cigarettes, and sure enough, they were missing. So rather than take up the carpet, he just mashed it down with his heel until it looked all right.

He then gathered up his tools and went to his van, and when he got inside, much to his surprise, his cigarettes were on the seat. As he was leaving a woman came to the door and called out to him, "Hey mister, I left the door to the bird cage open and I can't find my parakeet anywhere. Have you seen him?"

* * *

A golf fanatic got home after hitting eighteen holes one day and his wife asked him how it went. "Oh, it was just terrible," replied the duffer. "We were on the tenth tee when Harry had a heart attack and fell dead right there on the tee." "Oh my! That is terrible," said the wife. The man said, "Of course it was terrible! We still had nine holes to play, and it was just hit and drag Harry, hit and drag Harry..."

* * *

A man wandering on a deserted beach happened upon a bottle that had washed up on shore. He picked it up, dusted it off, and then uncorked it. When he did this a huge genie appeared. The genie said, "For freeing me from the bottle, I am going to give you three wishes, and you will have only five minutes to make them. But remember this, everything you wish for, your mother-in-law will get *double* what you ask for."

With that, the man thought for a minute and then said, "OK. For my first wish I wish for a million dollars." The genie obliged, a million dollars in cash appeared, and he said, "Alright, your mother-in-law will get two million."

The man then said, "For my second wish, I wish for a twenty-room mansion." Again, the genie obliged, and a twenty-room mansion appeared there on the waterfront overlooking the ocean. The Genie responded, "Alright, your mother-in-law will get a forty-room mansion right next door to you."

Finally, the man said, "Now, for my third wish, I want you to beat me *half* to death!"

* * *

A man planning to hike through the desert with some friends asked his doctor what precautions he should take. "If a rattlesnake bites you, you must immediately suck out all of the poison," he advised. The man said, "What if he bites me in a place I can't get to, like my tushy?" The doctor replied, "That's when you find out who your real friends are."

* * *

A truck driver pulled his rig into a truck stop. He got out, went inside, and ordered a cup of coffee, a hamburger, and a piece of pie. As the waitress set the food in front of him, three husky guys in leather jackets walked in. One took the coffee, one took the hamburger, and one took the piece of pie.

The truck driver got up, didn't say a word, and paid the waitress as he walked out. One of the guys in the leather jackets said to the waitress, "He wasn't much of a man, was he?" She said, "No, and he isn't much of a driver either. He just ran over three motorcycles with his truck!"

* * *

Two ants were sitting on the first tee of a country club when a not so gifted golfer was ready to tee off. One of the ants jumped on the ball and the second ant wanted to know why.

The first one answered, "I've seen him play and it's the last place he'd think of hitting."

* * *

A woman on a production line asked the plant manager for a raise. He said, "Your salary is already higher than any male worker out here and they all have families with two or three kids." "Look," she countered, "I thought we got paid for our production on the job, not for what we produce on our own time!"

* * *

A new waitress at a truck stop greasy spoon went over to a trucker's table to take his order. He ordered four tires, three headlights turned on, and four strips of rubber. The new waitress not really knowing what the man wanted, went back to the cook and repeated the order. The cook started laughing and said, "That means he wants four hot cakes, three eggs sunny side up, and four pieces of bacon."

The waitress nodded and proceeded to grab a can of chili beans and took them back out to the truck driver and put them on the table in front of him. The driver asked, "What are these for?" She replied, "I just thought you might want to gas up while you were waiting on your other truck parts!"

* * *

Two men were in a skyscraper wasting time when one man said to the other, "Watch this," and he proceeded to throw his watch out of a nearby window, run down thirty-five flights of stairs, and catch the watch before it ever hit the ground.

"That's nothing," said the other man who threw his watch out of the same window, walked down the thirty-five flights of stairs, ordered and ate a hot dog from a nearby street vendor, and eventually caught his watch before it hit the ground. His friend asked, "How on earth did you do that?" "Easy," replied the other man. "My watch is a half hour slow!"

* * *

Sarah Cannon was as much a part of television's elite society of talent as the country character she portrayed. She is seen here with Hollywood legend and friend, Dinah Shore.

In panic, a tired first-time traveler called down to the hotel's front desk shortly after checking in. "Help!" he yelled. "I'm trapped inside my room!" "What do you mean *trapped?*" asked the desk clerk. "Well, I see three doors," the man explained. "The first opens to a closet and the second to a bathroom. And the third door has a 'do not disturb sign' hanging on it!"

19.
All's Well That Ends Well

It could take a lifetime to rekindle the memories of the multitudes of friends and fans who have heard Minnie Pearl perform in an effort to collect more stories and jokes that she shared with them while she was with us. But who knows, maybe there's another bundle sitting down at the depot that everyone has forgotten about, hoping to eventually find it's way from the Switch to the presses—somewhere down the line. For now, I guess it would be safe to say that Minnie probably told or heard them all.

As for life in Grinder's Switch, I'm sure that the residents there miss having her around to recount the everyday trials and tribulations of their small town with big ideas. In the meantime, they may simply be waiting for some other bard to rejoin their lives already in progress, and carry their chronicles to the big city or perhaps down to the next stop on the afternoon run.

So if you happen to be taking a Sunday drive in the country and stumble upon a small community in the middle of nowhere, keep an eye out for train tracks. When you find some, follow them in any direction you please. But if you suddenly come upon a turnoff in the nickel-plated straight rails, take a good look around. You may be right in the middle of Grinder's Switch.

Most likely you've merely discovered a crossing that marks one of the thousands of tiny rural towns that have their own brothers and sisters, country doctors, and local gossips. They certainly will have their own mountain hermits and farm gentlemen, too. I'm also convinced that you'll sense a lot of the Switch in these places. But no matter how hard you look, and no matter how long you try, I doubt that you'll find another Minnie Pearl.

Even so, when you jump out of your big city sedan and hit the streets for a walk around, be sure to greet the townspeople appropriately. Give them a big "Howdee! I'm just so proud to be here," and see how they answer. It shouldn't come as any surprise.

Courtesy of Hope Powell Photography

A lifetime of comedy earned "Cousin" Minnie Pearl her place of honor in the Country Music Hall of Fame in 1975.